PILGRIMAGE FROM KNOWN TO UNKNOWN

AND

THE MEDITATION ECHNIQUES OF LORD SHIVA

(THE EARLIEST, PRE-HISTORIC MEDITATION TECHNIQUES OF ANCIENT INDIA)

DEDICATED TO MY HUSBAND Sri K C N Nair WHO IS NOW NO MORE

By

Dr (Mrs)Shantha N Nair

ACKNOWLEDGMENT

The invisible spirit of my husband Sri K C N Nair, who is now no more, the presence of which and whom, I feel and experience every moment in my life now, as before, when he was alive, and as usual, guided me, helped me and made me write this book from the start till the finish. May the ALMIGHTY take me to him at the earliest without any further delay, so that I, becoming the spirit like him, reunite with him forever.

The entire credit of this book, however, goes to my son-Uday Gowri Shankar who induced me, encouraged me and finally requested me along with my daughter-in-law Roopa to resume my hobby of writing books. I had decided to put a big full stop to many of my activities as I lost all interest, enthusiasm and spirit that was uppermost in me throughout my life till then. My grandchildren also played an important role in this and finally, I decided to write this book. My grandson Pranav Shankar and my granddaughter Gayathri Shankar very happily and enthusiastically extended all necessary technical help whenever I needed and this book is the outcome of all their combined efforts. May the ALMIGHTY guide all of them, be with them in all their endeavours and bless all of them throughout always and always.

PILGRIMAGE FROM KNOWN TO UNKNOWN AND THE MEDITATION TECHNIQUES OF LORD SHIVA

CONTENTS

<u>PART----1</u>

THE PILGRIMAGE FROM THE KNOWN TO THE UNKNOWN

The term Pilgrimage usually refers to the journey that is undertaken physically, to a place or places, already known or yet to be known to the pilgrim, that is far or near and most importantly, has great religious or spiritual significance, and that can be reached either by walking through the distance, especially if the sacred place is located on a mountain or hill that cannot be reached except on foot or utilizing any vehicle or transport system that will take the pilgrim to his desired destination or destinations. It is possible for the pilgrim who has gone through the journey to explain and describe the various places, places of worship and their religious and spiritual significance, the climate there, the languages spoken in the place, the people and their beliefs, customs, festivals, their food patterns, their activities and so on and his experiences as well from the time he started the journey until his return, for the benefit of others. One can also go through this journey either alone or in groups. Also, this type of pilgrimage need not necessarily be a one-time journey as it can be undertaken once a lifetime or several times depending upon the capacity and desire of the pilgrim concerned.

THE SPIRITUAL PILGRIMAGE

The Pilgrimage from the known to the unknown that this book deals with and that at its best is only a very small and humble attempt to enhance human well-being is not a physical journey that is undertaken entirely physically and externally but is an inward, mental journey, a journey of our mind that is both physical as well as subtle, towards our Soul, that is subtle, to reach the ultimate single destination- the spiritual wisdom that is the supreme and ultimate goal of humans. It is essentially a quest to realise who one essentially is, that is, to realise "WHO AM I" and then finally reap all the miraculous benefits that such a journey unfolds. It is also a journey from the known, in this case, of the mind or the thought process towards an unknown destination about which one has no clue, in the sense, that although he might have heard or is knowledgeable about that state of spiritual wisdom either directly from an enlightened being or indirectly from discourses of the spiritually advanced souls or might have gained that knowledge through his reading and understanding of the ancient scriptures, yet he has no subjective experience of what happens to him, the spiritual seeker, ultimately when he reaches the spiritual destination, that is- when one gains spiritual enlightenment or wisdom that results in unlimited and extensive happiness, peace and the ultimate freedom to oneself which is the very goal and destination of any spiritual process. The spiritual destination is also neither visible nor external, physical or gross that can be explained and described but is something which can only be experienced by the spiritually enlightened being.

As in the case of the usual pilgrimage in this spiritual journey also there are several paths to reach the destination that can be termed as methods or ways. In this pilgrimage, unlike the usual pilgrimage where one has to follow any particular route mostly, except for diversions here and there, in this journey it is up to the pilgrim to choose any single path or also a combination of two or more spiritual paths or methods as per his liking that is governed by his inherent and fundamental nature or qualities and as per his capacity to understand and practise. Some methods are difficult to understand and follow and some others are comparatively easy, some methods are roundabout, certain other methods are like shortcuts, some paths the pilgrim may like more when compared to some other paths and so on. The spiritual seeker can make use of his intellect aspect of the mind which is known as the path of knowledge or he can choose the path of selfless and dedicated service by making use of his organs of the body like hands and legs particularly, which are considered as organs of action and that is activated by the mind, or he can make use of the mind in its emotional aspect, particularly the divine emotion of unconditional love, trust and surrender towards God or the Almighty, as in the case of the path of devotion, or he can make use of his mind directly as in the case of Dhyana yoga that is the path of meditation. Dhyana yoga refers to meditation in which one can make use of his energy. There are also various types of meditations like the Chakra meditation that is, the meditation on the subtle wheels of energy in our body, the meditation that is found in the eight-limbed Yoga of sage Patanjali, Kriya yoga is a meditation technique that makes use of Pranayama that is generally interpreted as breath control, and there are also meditation techniques that make use of Tantras, mantras and yantras and so on. The number of meditation techniques is also increasing in modern times and it is also becoming more and more popular day by day. This book particularly deals with the path of meditation.

The vehicle that is used for transporting the pilgrim to his destination that is a place, is operated either with Petrol, diesel, or electrical energy, or the pilgrim can reach the final point with the help of horses or camels, or ponies or even can be carried by humans themselves, or the pilgrim can also walk the distance and reach the destination. In the spiritual pilgrimage, there is no physical distance between the starting point and the destination, since the vehicle, that is the mind and the destination, that is, reaching and merging with the Soul that resides in the cave of our own heart, and also the Universal Consciousness or Soul are both inside us, although the mind and the Soul are invisible to us. The individual Soul is nothing but the

Universal Soul or Consciousness that is present in every creation. However, the destination will seem to be far away for the one who is not spiritually inclined.

Though the vehicle and the destination look different from each other at the beginning of the spiritual journey, in its final stage, they become the same because the mind then gets dissolved in the Spirit or Soul without any trace of the existence of its own and then the Spirit or the Soul or consciousness or the Awareness only remains but nothing else. Then the pilgrim whose mind has merged with the Soul automatically merges with the Universal Supreme Consciousness and he becomes the same as the Supreme, the all-pervading and all-enveloping Supreme consciousness itself. It is like the small bubble that appears from the waves of the ocean disappearing into the ocean itself after bursting and merging itself with the water of the ocean losing all its separate identity. In this journey, once the ultimate destination is reached then that is final and no more such journeys need to be undertaken by the pilgrim. He becomes a different person altogether as he has reached a different dimension, in which he becomes a man of wisdom or an enlightened being- the very universal consciousness or soul, or the Spirit, or God himself or itself that is nothing but the Universal energy itself, that is an embodiment of all perfection, is omnipotent, omniscient and omnipresent, eternal, pure and so on. It is a one-time inner journey of one's mind in which the mind that is the invisible vehicle takes one to the desired goal that is also invisible.

Such a spiritual pilgrimage is beneficial both for the spiritually inclined one and for the one who is worldly without any spiritual ambition of knowing the eternal truth. The worldly being who undertakes this journey in a sincere and committed manner, at least up to a certain point, even if he does not continue the journey up to the last stage or destination due to some reason or the other will also be rewarded with good physical health and mental happiness and peace. He will also become a good human being with many positive qualities. In short, while living he will become a blessed being. But once a man realises his goal or reaches his ultimate destination then what he experiences is nothing but pure and permanent joy in which he becomes blissful always whatever may be the situations, circumstances, and happenings in his life whether they are categorised as either good or bad by others. It is not because he has no emotions whatsoever. He will be the one who will be the most compassionate, kind, loving and so on. He will be one whose very nature is compassion, love and so on. Such a person will also feel the pain and sorrow of others as his own. Whether it is the physical pain or mental sorrow of himself or that of others he will be able to overcome it in no time because of his wisdom and awareness that one is not the body or mind but is essentially the soul that does not get affected by any happenings of life. Even his very face will reveal his inner peace. This is because his wisdom makes him view everything as the same and as equal. Such a state however can only be experienced by one. Worldly happenings including any physical pain or mental agony that usually affect others will have no impact upon him because he has become one who has realised, that, he as a being is not his body and mind that are only his belongings and that get influenced and affected by the so-called good and bad in life but is essentially the Spirit or consciousness or the Soul in him that cannot be touched by the dualities of life. This will make him go beyond any type of physical pain and mental suffering. Such a realised being, goes beyond all dualities of life like good and bad, pain and pleasure, heat and cold, happiness and misery and so on. He also starts viewing everything and everyone as the same because he has a balanced mind. He also becomes one who has understood and experienced within himself the supreme reality or truth that all creation is only a true reflection and a part of the Universal Consciousness.

He sees all creation in him and himself in all the other creations.

The spiritually enlightened man will look and behave outwardly like any other person in this world, but with the inner realisation that these outward things are only a show in which he has to play a part. That means though he gets involved, he does not get entangled in any of them as he starts viewing everything that goes on in this world as a mere show and as child's play. Such an attitude releases him from all bondages and entanglements of life. He will have no attachment towards anything in the world whether they are objects, people, situations and so on because he has become one who is detached from all worldly things. He starts viewing everything from a distance like a witness or an observer. This does not mean that he does not cherish or enjoy the good things in the world. He enjoys them all with the full awareness that such enjoyments are neither important nor lasting. He will be a person who accepts every situation in life as it comes. He never discriminates against anything as good or bad. He will treat all situations, people, objects and experiences that are connected to this world as the same or equal. This gives him total freedom and permanent bliss. Usually one becomes very happy physically, and mentally at one moment and when situations, objects and people are not as per his liking then one suffers. Since the enlightened being is not attached to his body and mind he also gets detached from everything in this world and that makes him enjoy freedom, peace and happiness permanently because there is no duality of perception at that stage. He becomes an embodiment of pure and permanent joy that can only be experienced but cannot be expressed as one has to experience it for himself and one can realise it only through one's own subjective experience. This pilgrimage is a lone journey that one must undertake for realising the ultimate supreme Reality, which is the very purpose and goal of all human beings in which one can enjoy permanent freedom by getting freed from all sorrows and sufferings of worldly life.

The spiritually enlightened man, while living in this world becomes the most joyful and peaceful man exhibiting positive qualities like kindness, compassion, love and so on. His words and acts may even look crazy to ordinary_people because he cannot be understood by ordinary minds._He has no negativity in him, and this makes him lovable. Positivity becomes his very nature, and he is not only a good being, but he is an embodiment of purity. A good man also has good qualities like love, kindness, compassion etc. But an enlightened person goes even beyond goodness as he becomes goodness itself. For example, such a pure one is not only compassionate like a good man who is endowed with all good qualities but he is also the very quality of compassion because he has transcended even goodness and has become purity itself. When he loves and is kind and compassionate and so on to others, it is not because he thinks that these are good qualities and that he will be rewarded for these qualities someday or other. He does not bother or have such slightest thoughts even. And this is the difference between a good person who has good and positive qualities in him and an enlightened or a man of spiritual wisdom. As per the ancient Indian spirituality and belief system, an enlightened spiritual being can go beyond repeated cycles of birth and death as he gets merged with the very source of creation. A good man, on the other hand, it is said in spirituality, will be born again to enjoy the benefits of his good deeds. That means if one has to get Liberation from the repeated cycles of birth and death then one has to go beyond the three qualities of nature which are goodness, passion and ignorance. Then only it is possible. Such a man of wisdom is also respected and cherished by one and all alike. His aura which is the subtle energy that surrounds his physical body automatically attracts all from far and near. In the Sanskrit language that was spoken throughout ancient India, Aura is called Thejas or Ojas, which is the heat and the light energy in a spiritually enlightened being. This gives rise to a glow that is visible not only on the face of the person but also all over the body of the enlightened being. It is said even fragrance will emanate from the body of such a man of Spiritual Wisdom. The spiritually enlightened being is supposed to have a pronounced Aura. Swami Vivekananda says the enhanced Aura gives a tremendous power of attraction, glow and vitality. It is compared to the radiance that surrounds the soothing and cool light of the moon. Such a being also radiates and spreads happiness and peace to all those who come into contact with him. It is understood from the scriptures and also seen from the life of the extraordinary men of wisdom that they get unimaginable powers and whatever they wish and utter come true. However, their extraordinary powers will be used only for the welfare of one and all. The spiritually enlightened being becomes aware of Awareness or is conscious of the Consciousness itself. Once such a being sheds his body, it is told in the Scriptures that he will go beyond the repeated cycles of birth and death. That means, he as the consciousness, will never go through the repeated births and deaths again. He will become immortal. This is Liberation, Freedom, Mukti or Nirvana.

The role of the mind in the spiritual journey

The ultimate purpose and goal of the spiritual journey, whatever may be the path, or the method followed by one, is to attain spiritual wisdom or enlightenment although this journey also benefits one with physical health and mental well-being. Any spiritual method essentially makes use of the mind that is subtly located inside the physical body. Although we cannot see the mind that is within us, we can however understand the way it works within our body through our thought process. The mind is nothing but a series of thoughts. The physical body is gross hence there is no difficulty for us to see it and observe it externally. The ultimate goal of any spiritual process is to become spiritually enlightened by making use of the mind. The physical body plays an important role in this journey because the vehicle or the means, that is, how we can go through this journey, namely, the mind can also be called the thoughts or thought process which is located inside our physical body. The mind by itself and also by making use of the organs of senses and the organs of actions of the body, like a vehicle, is capable to carry on the spiritual journey.

Mind is said to be the Lord of all sensory organs and it is the one that directs them to perform their respective functions. The senses collect the necessary knowledge or information from the outside world and pass them on to the mind for further processing inside us. In this sense both our body and mind play a very big role in the spiritual process and their importance can never be underestimated because if the spiritual journey has to be undertaken it has to make use of the vehicle namely the mind that is in the body of beings. All spiritual methods make use of the mind either directly or indirectly to reach the destination of spiritual wisdom. The scriptures compare the body, mind and

Soul to the temple, the sanctum sanctorum and the Deity installed there. While the body is compared to the temple structure, the mind is supposed to be the sanctum sanctorum which is called the Garbha Gruha or the womb that is a very small room and dark without windows and the Deity is installed at the centre, and is most important is compared to the very Soul or the Spirit or the Awareness or Consciousness in beings.

The mind that is our inner instrument is both gross as well as subtle. It is therefore known as a subtle matter. It is not physical or tangible or gross like our physical body. We cannot assess its magnitude or its location in our body. Just as each person is different physically, so also each one is different in their mental makeup as well. A strong mind can influence and overpower a weak mind just as a strong body can overpower a weak body.

Consciousness in the sense of Supreme awareness or Supreme intelligence is the Universal energy that one can realise only through the mind ultimately. Mind is nothing but the thought process. Thoughts are the basis of the mind. Hence when thoughts cease the mind also disappears as it merges with the Supreme Consciousness or the Supreme Awareness.

It is said that the mind that is a powerful instrument inside us is both a demon as well a Divine. It is because the mind is made up of and therefore has all three qualities namely, goodness, then passion and activity and lastly lethargy and ignorance. The goodness makes one a Satvik person, that is a good human being even to the extent of being divine.

Usually, all people who have more positivity in them belong to this category. Rajasik nature in one makes him passionate, very active and so on. This nature we find in warriors, leaders and rulers and so on. They have many positive as well as negative qualities in them. Those who are always lethargic and ignorant are those who have very many negative qualities in them. All three qualities are inherent in every human being and a person is categorised as Satvik or good or Rajasic or passionate or Thamasik or lethargic depending upon which quality or qualities are dominating in them. When a person is Satvik then he becomes divine and if he is full of negativities and is therefore Thamasik in nature, then, he will be acting like a demon with an evil and antisocial mindset.

The one who is on the spiritual path should understand the mind first then transform it and then finally transcend it to reach the desired destination of Spiritual enlightenment. For purpose of understanding, we can view the mind at its two levels- the lower mind and the higher mind. The lower mind is the emotional mind with all emotions and feelings, positive and negative qualities. It also makes the senses function and perceives all types of information. But it also tries to overpower us depending upon the nature of the individual. However, the lower mind which is the mind that is at its lower level with all its expectations, possessiveness etc. that are negative qualities along with its positive qualities has its role to play in worldly life. But it can also make us aware of its higher level through the spiritual process. We can know the ultimate Truth only through the lower mind. The higher mind is the transformed lower mind. It is the same mind that goes beyond the lower mind after getting purified with noble words, thoughts and deeds and becomes one with the Supreme Soul or Consciousness. Once the lower mind gets transformed to a higher level then, the lower mind disappears automatically because it has no more role to play. Then the mind that is transformed as the higher mind only remains as Awareness or the all-pervading Consciousness. After all, the purpose of any spiritual process is to transform the mind, that is to purify the mind from its impurities and lift it from its lower level to the higher level. It is just like carbon after undergoing very many processes underneath the earth becoming a diamond. Although diamond was originally carbon, still no one will call carbon a diamond. Only when the carbon gets transformed after a long period within the soil it can become a diamond, but not otherwise. Just as the transformed carbon becomes a diamond later, after a very long period, similarly the same mind that was at its lower level, after long and arduous spiritual practises gets transformed into the higher mind. After some time, in the course of the spiritual process, the transformed mind disappears altogether. This is the stage when one transcends the mind. The transformed mind that later disappears, by getting united with the Supreme Consciousness becomes the same as the Supreme or Universal Consciousness. During the spiritual process, the thoughts or the lower mind gradually begins to disappear and after some time the lower mind disappears and, in its place, the transformed higher mind that merges with the Supreme Consciousness losing all its separate identity comes and becomes the same as the Supreme Consciousness. It is like the river that originates from any hilltop or mountain top flowing through several places and paths finally entering and merging into the ocean and then it is no more a river but a part of the vast expansive ocean only. Once the river merges with the ocean then it is not possible to differentiate the river water from the water of the ocean. Similarly in the final point or climax of the spiritual process, all thoughts disappear and the mind without the support of thoughts also disappears because for its very existence mind needs thoughts. This is the state when one goes beyond the mind and merges with the Universal Consciousness and becomes That.

The lower mind or the emotional mind has its limitations, and boundaries and also is exclusive. The transformed mind which is the higher mind, on the other hand, has no limitation, it is boundless and all-inclusive. If one can subjugate one's lower mind then it will think, speak and act through the organs of senses and action, totally in a divine manner. On the other hand, if the mind becomes the master, then it will drag us towards doom because then one's thoughts, words and actions also can become devilish. However, it is the same mind that was once, that is before its transformation, seen as the lower mind that gets transformed into the higher mind or Self. It is the same mind but at different levels. So, the one who is on the spiritual path should, first of all, understand the nature of our mind and the second step is to transform the mind so that the mind becomes good and then pure. When the mind becomes pure it will entertain only divine thoughts, words and deeds. At that point the mind automatically will go beyond all negative and worldly thoughts, words and deeds and then all thoughts will disappear and it attains the transcendental state of the Supreme Consciousness in which one becomes the Universal Consciousness itself. Meditation which is the basis for any spiritual method also speeds up the process of transformation and ultimately it takes one to the transcendental state of Supreme Consciousness. On the other hand, if one becomes the slave of the lower mind without any understanding of the mind then the mind will drag us like a rudderless boat and will spell doom to that person. In chapter 6 verse 5 of Bhagavad Geetha, Lord Krishna says that one's mind is one's friend as well as his enemy. In the same chapter in verse 6, He says, that the one who can subjugate his senses and emotions through his mind, which he calls the lower Self, becomes his friend and helps him in realising his very inner Self (the higher Self or the higher Mind) or the Soul that is in him and that is only a reflection of the Supreme Soul or Consciousness, through one-pointed meditation. It is like the butter getting transformed into ghee and becoming the ghee, once the butter goes through the process of heating. The very basis of ghee is milk. Milk after a certain process becomes curd. Curd after undergoing a certain process gets transformed into buttermilk. From the butter, milk butter is taken and the last stage is when the butter becomes ghee. However, the butter by itself without undergoing the process of heating cannot be called ghee because the butter should become devoid of all its impurities to become the ghee. On the other hand, when the lower Self or mind starts dominating then the same mind becomes his enemy and destroys him. Therefore, one has to conquer the lower mind through knowledge of the Higher Self that is the higher mind, the Supreme Consciousness.

Mind is like a very sharp instrument that can be used to take the life of one if it is in the hands of a murderer or to save the life of one if it is in the hands of a surgeon. The mind can also be compared to a double-edged weapon because it can make a person a devil or divine. It can create opposites like happiness or misery, positivity or negativity and so on. It is even said that what we think we become. All different emotions are only the different states of mind. Mind is also compared to a monkey as it jumps from one thought to the other very quickly. The mind is also considered the lord of all the senses as it directs the five organs of senses namely the eyes that see, ears that hear, the nose that smells, the tongue that tastes, and skin that feels the touch, and also the organs of actions namely the mouth that is the organ of speech, the two hands, the two legs, the organs of excretion and the organ of reproduction to perform their functions.

When an individual is at the peak of any positive emotion then he gets a glimpse of his higher mind. However, it does not last long. One who is in deep love or when one is at the peak of the quality of compassion becomes the same as that quality and at that time he even forgets himself. At this point man becomes divine –the Consciousness itself. But very soon his emotions change and he becomes a very ordinary being with many negative qualities. It is like one who gets identified with the hero or the heroine in a movie that he or she is engrossed with. However, this identification disappears as soon as the movie is over and he becomes the same one he was before. The identification in this case is temporary. But in the case of an enlightened being the positive qualities become permanent in him and he also becomes those very positive qualities permanently without falling from that higher level. For such a being the lower mind is no more. Only the higher mind as Consciousness remains always permanently because the mind at its higher-level merges with the Soul or Spirit or the Universal Awareness or Consciousness. However, such an experience is beyond any explanation or description as one can know it only experientially. Such Awareness comes intuitively all of a sudden, in a split second even without one's knowing unexpectedly. Even in worldly life all inventions and discoveries happened finally in a split second only after a prolonged, committed intense and wholehearted effort on the part of the researcher.

The ancient sages of India identified different aspects of the mind as per its state of awareness, its qualities, its level, and as per its functions. They stated that there are five states of mind as per the mind's level of awareness. These are the conscious mind, the unconscious mind, the sub-Conscious mind, the super Conscious mind and finally the supra-Conscious mind. When we are fully conscious or aware then we become fully conscious of all our thoughts, words and deeds. In the unconscious mind, the thought process that results in words and deeds happens automatically without any conscious effort. In this state the brain or intellect functions at its lowest frequency. The subconscious mind is the seat of memory and past experiences in life. It is also the seat of all deep-rooted or submerged and suppressed thoughts and emotions. In the Superconscious state of mind, one gets transformed from being body-mind conscious to the level being spirit conscious. One goes beyond all dualities of life. The final state of mind is the Supra Conscious state in which one goes beyond the mind and is not aware of his Self also. This is the state of enlightenment when one becomes an embodiment of permanent, total Bliss.

As per its qualities mind is categorised into three different qualities. The quality of goodness that is called Sattvik, the quality of passion and action that is, the Rajasik, and the quality of lethargy and ignorance that is, Tamasik. Sattvik qualities are predominant in the case of spiritually advanced souls like saints and sages, Rajasik qualities are mostly found in warriors and kings while the Tamasik quality dominates people who are ignorant, lazy and disillusioned. However, all three qualities one can see in most people generally and people are categorised as good or passionate or ignorant depending upon which quality or qualities are dominant in them.

The ancient seers viewed the mind in its different states or levels also. In the waking state the mind, through the sensory organs of the body perceives all external objects. Both body and mind are active in this state. In the dreaming state, the mind goes beyond space and time but is active and creates the dream world but the body becomes inactive. In the deep sleep state where there are no dreams both mind and body become inactive. The mind at this stage becomes soul Conscious. It is like one who is in a coma stage, that is when he is not conscious of anything including his body and mind. This state is often called temporary death because one becomes aware of himself only after he wakes up from his sleep. Beyond these three states, the ancient sages of India also identified two more states of Consciousness. These were termed by them as Thuriya and Thuriyatheetha. It is said that in the state of Thuriya one gets a glimpse of his real Self that is, not as body or mind but as the pure Soul. But in Thuriyatheetha one is supposed to experience only Bliss but nothing else. He even forgets himself and it is said that in that state he becomes Bliss itself.

Mind is also supposed to be having four functional aspects. These four aspects are Manas which is the emotional mind where all emotional thoughts and feelings arise, Buddhi or intellect which is the rational and discriminatory mind where the thoughts are analysed logically through reasoning, which is highly useful for worldly life, then the Chittha, that can be interpreted as the Subconscious mind that is the storehouse of all thoughts that are based upon the memories of the past and information that are gathered and had settled down deep inside this storehouse. This is a very important aspect of the mind. It is said that it stores memories of one's past births also that can be brought to the conscious mind by enlightened beings. Many interpret the term Chittha as the very Consciousness. But the Supreme Consciousness is not Chittha but it is Chit. Usually, the state of enlightenment is described as Sat-Chit- Ananda which is the ultimate reality or Truth – Consciousness –Bliss. Chittha is supposed to be the base from where all thoughts of the past arise. Sage Patanjali says the very goal of Yoga is Chittha Vruthi Nirodha which means the elimination of all thoughts. In this Chittha refers to thoughts but not the ultimate Supreme Consciousness or the Universal Soul. The fourth aspect of the mind is Ahamkara which is the ego-sense in one that gives rise to the feeling or the thought of 'I' and 'mine. Even animals have this sense and it is highly pronounced in humans. Everyone knows what it means because unless one is spiritually enlightened the rest of all have the ego sense in them in a lesser or greater measure.

Intellect and Intelligence

The Supreme Consciousness-the supreme intelligence in beings is however not the intellect but it is the Intelligence or Awareness. Intellect is rational, discriminatory, analytical and logical which is useful for carrying on worldly life mostly. But intelligence is that which is beyond intellect and also transcendental and that transforms one from being human to the level of becoming divine. This gives rise to intuition. The sages of the past could realise, very many things about the Universe and creation, intuitively, while in meditation. It is beyond intellect that is reasoning and logical analysis.

Awareness

In Indian Spirituality Supreme Consciousness or Intelligence, or the universal, vast, expansive consciousness is equated with Awareness. Awareness in this sense goes beyond being conscious or becoming aware of the external world, of our body and mind and so on. Its meaning extends even further and it is equated with the very Supreme Consciousness.

Intelligence or the sense of Awareness that is Consciousness is found in the entire creation whether it is movable or not. Awareness or Consciousness is mostly submerged in other creations. It is only in humans that is most pronounced. It is stated that even inanimate mountains grow. Only where Awareness or Consciousness is, we find growth. For example, it is found, that Himalayas which is the youngest mountain range in the world grows, although it is not visible to the naked eye. In the case of plants, trees etc. we can see their growth. The Awareness or the Consciousness or the Intelligence in them makes them grow and they bend and grow towards the sunlight. The Awareness or the Consciousness in them makes creepers bend towards some support. The level of Consciousness in the animate world is still higher but, the insects, birds and animals are aware or are Conscious of only two things namely survival and procreation. They just eat, drink, sleep and procreate and that is the goal of their life. All their activities are only towards fulfilling these two purposes or goals of life. Even in the case of ants, we see them flocking towards sugar, ignoring the salt that is placed nearby. But in the case of humans who are considered the highest species on the ladder of creation, the level of Consciousness is at its highest and it is also highly pronounced. As humans, our purpose in life is not limited to merely maintaining and safeguarding our life and procreation but we have a higher goal that is lasting, supreme and imperishable and that is the realisation of the Supreme Consciousness that is the Universal Consciousness. Even a very worldly person after acquiring everything that he wished for in his life and tasting success in life always craves for something more in life, something beyond worldly happiness that would give him permanent joy and peace. At that stage, he realises that worldly happiness and success are not everything in life as they are not permanent but transitory and all worldly happiness ultimately brings only physical ill health and mental sorrows in the form of tension, stress, anxiety etc. and he turns his attention and goes in search of permanent joy and peace within himself through some spiritual means or the other. This is the case for all human beings although there can be exceptions.

If all human beings understand what is meant by the spiritual journey and undertake this journey by practising any of the methods of their choice and belief, at least up to a certain extent if not to the level of ultimate spiritual enlightenment then the entire world undoubtedly will become heaven on earth because, then, there will be harmonious living in the world with a live and let live attitude, where there is no hatred or jealousy, war or crime but only peace and happiness in which every human being enjoys not only physical and mental health but also spiritual wellbeing.

WHAT IS SOUL OR SPIRIT OR CONSCIOUSNESS AND THE FEATURES OF AN ENLIGHTENED BEING OR A MAN OF WISDOM

According to the ancient sages of India, the all-pervading, vast expansive Consciousness of the Universe that is also known as the Universal Consciousness, or the Cosmic Soul or Spirit or energy, Awareness or Intelligence is the Seed of the Universe and the entire creation. It is that which created this Universe along with the Cosmic Nature that is endowed with the fundamental three qualities of Nature, upholds all creation and dissolves the entire creation for a new beginning, that is, for a new cycle of the creation process.

The ancient scriptures state that the Universal Soul represents masculine energy while the Cosmic Nature represents female energy. They are not different from each other as both these are only energy. This is very clearly represented by the concept of Ardha(half) Nareeshwara (Naree means female and Eeshwara means the God in which Lord Shiva's physical body is partly male representing the masculine and His other half is female that represents Goddess Parvathi who is supposed to be Lord Shiva's consort.) The two energy channels that are represented by the two subtle Nadis or channels in our body, which are known as the Ida and Pingala Nadi also represent the masculine and the feminine energy in one being. It is said that one becomes a male or a female depending upon which energy is dominating one. These Nadis run along the spine. In between these two channels or Nadis, at the centre, there is another

Nadi that also goes along the Spine. This is called the Sushumna Nadi or Brahma Nadi which is supposed to be the central channel or Nadi (through which the vital Energy flows) of the Absolute Consciousness. The ancient sages put forth these revelations on the basis, that, what is true in the Microcosm is also true in the Macrocosm.

The entire creation partakes the three qualities of Nature. The three fundamental qualities of Nature are, broadly, the nature of Goodness, secondly that of passion and also activity and third ignorance, delusion, and lethargy. Even before birth, that is, when the child is in the womb of its mother, the cosmic energy in the form of the individual Soul that is in Sanskrit known as the Purusha meaning the one who resides within the body of a being, together with the Cosmic Nature that is referred to as Prakriti with its three qualities enters into the body of a being. Depending upon the quality, or, the qualities that dominate one, one performs in the world as and when he grows. The thoughts, words and deeds of a person will depend upon which quality or qualities are dominant in one.

The all-pervading Soul or the Spirit that enters into the body of a being is referred to as the individual Soul. It is like when the potter makes a pot, the air gets into the pot. Although the air inside the pot is not different from the air outside the pot, still the air inside the pot gets limited because it is inside the pot. However, the air that is inside the pot is not in any way different from the air outside it as it is only a portion of the outside air that has got into the pot. It does not get affected by the qualities of the pot-whether the pot is smooth or rough, whether it is made up of mud or plastic and so on. Once the pot breaks then the air that was hitherto limited to the inside of the pot that has a physical boundary as per its shape, merges into the air outside without any difference.

The Soul or the Spirit of the individual is independent and it also does not partake the qualities of the individual who exhibits a combination of all the three qualities of Nature or the Cosmos in different proportions and it is also non-perishable and eternal. At the time of death, that is, when the Prana or the Life energy goes out of the body then, the individual Soul that is in the body of the beings becomes one with the Universal Soul. Prana or breath itself is not the Soul. The Soul is that Vital energy which activates the Prana. This is the case with the entire creation starting from the lowest species to the highest species namely humans.

The Supreme Consciousness or the Universal Soul or Spirit is also referred to as the Supreme Awareness. In the ordinary sense the term awareness means being conscious of our body or mind and their state, the worldly things and activities and so on that are perishable and therefore are not immortal. If a person becomes unconscious then we say that he is not conscious. But in Spirituality, the term Consciousness or Awareness refers to the Universal Soul or Spirit itself and also that state of a being when one becomes aware/ experiences the fact that he and the Universal Soul or the Consciousness, that is, the intelligence or the awareness in him are not different from each other but are the same. In the enlightened state one automatically, without any effort on his part, experiences that Awareness. In such a super Conscious state he experiences that unity that he and the Universal Self that is also referred to as the Divine, or Super Soul or Universal Consciousness or God are the same without any difference. This state of enlightenment happens to the spiritually advanced Souls all of a sudden like a revelation.

By making use of the mind directly or indirectly, that is inside the body, one realises what he, in reality, is, that is, whether he is mere, a physical body that is gross and/or the mind that is called as subtle matter because it is both gross and also subtle. As and when one progresses in his spiritual journey it becomes clear to him that he essentially is not the body or his mind that are only perishable but the pure Soul or Spirit, or Consciousness or even what we may call Awareness that resides in the core of his heart as the individual Soul, that is eternal or imperishable and is invisible.

We can understand only a few features of the soul from the ancient scriptures, where the ancient sages of India called the Rishis have revealed their subjective experiences regarding what is Soul. However, the experience that one enjoys at that stage when one merges his Self with the very Universal Self or Soul or Spirit or the Universal energy or the very Consciousness, the Supreme intelligence or God cannot be described or explained fully and effectively as one can know that state of Pure Bliss only by experiencing it by himself. At the most one can only get some idea about the Soul and also about the Ultimate experience of those who had gained the ultimate wisdom by unifying their Consciousness with the Universal Soul, from those who have realised and enjoyed such a transcendental State. It is like knowing about mango fruit is possible through explanations and descriptions about the mango fruit but the real taste of the mango one experiences only by tasting it.

The innumerable ancient scriptures of India, particularly the Vedas and also the Upanishads which form the end portion of the Vedas, and that is supposed to be the crown of all Vedas, and also the sacred scripture Bhagavad Geetha that contains the essence of the teachings found in the Upanishads, and that narrate Lord Krishna's (supposed to be the complete incarnation of Lord Vishnu who was one of the trinity of Gods) messages to mankind through Arjuna, a prince, reveal to us the features of the Soul and also the marks of an enlightened being.

A few of the statements of the spiritually enlightened Rishis or sages of ancient India found in the verses of some of the Vedas and Upanishads and also Bhagavad Geetha about the Soul and the marks of an enlightened being are given below. The following statements were made by the enlightened sages in their supra-Conscious state of enlightenment where only intelligence and intuition remained but not intellect and reasoning or logic and therefore may seem to be beyond the comprehension of ordinary beings like us who are yet to experience that state.

A FEW FEATURES OF THE SOUL AS PER SOME OF THE VEDAS AND UPANISHADS

Rig Veda

1. The supreme soul makes all that is and that shall be.
2. The Universe was in the navel of the universal Consciousness where in abide all manifested things
3. No one can find Him, the Absolute Soul that created everything.
4. The Supreme Soul has innumerable heads, eyes, feet and so on. He or that Energy pervades every side of the Universe. It or that energy fills the entire space. (Indicating the all-pervasive nature of the Supreme Consciousness)
5. All creation forms only one-fourth of the all-pervading Consciousness

the remaining three-fourths remain eternal all over space.

Yajur Veda –Shukla Yajur Veda

1. The Universal Consciousness or Soul has eyes, mouth, arms, and feet on all sides. He is the God who created this Universe and He protects all and every creation of His with His arms as wings. (This description is symbolic)
2. You cannot find Him, the creator, as He is formless.
3. He, the all-pervading Self with His self enters into the body of all as the inner soul of beings.

Atharva Veda

1. Whoever knows the Truth knows that all beings are nothing but that Self within one's own body.

Upanishads

Rig Veda Upanishads

Aitareya Upanishad

1. All creatures that move or fly and those which do not move have Consciousness. All these are impelled by Consciousness. The Universe has Consciousness as its eye and Consciousness is its end, Consciousness is the Universal Soul.
2. This Universe is nothing but Consciousness. From Him, all creation originates and unto Him, all get dissolved and by Himself they are maintained.

Atma Bodha Upanishad

1. The Soul resides in the heart of the Lotus.

2. I, the inner self, am without any positive or negative. I am the everlasting Bliss, the witness, and am independent; with no old age or decay or duality; pure knowledge and the ocean of Liberation. I am subtle without attributes, without the three qualities of Nature (The Sattvic which is goodness; Rajasic, which is Passionate, and Tamasic which is ignorance and delusion). All worlds exist in me; I am the changeless Consciousness that is beyond reason and action. I am unborn, pure, real, the endless knowledge, auspicious, indivisible, faultless, pure Bliss, ever shining, without beginning and an end, and also the knower of Truth. I am without a second,

the Consciousness, which is the basis of the Universe. I am pervaded by Bliss. I have no desire for the things of the world. (These are the words of a sage who has become the very Universal Supreme Energy or Consciousness)

3. The Sun that makes the pot shine is not destroyed along with the pot. Similarly, the spirit or the Soul or the Consciousness is not destroyed along with the body.
4. Realising this Truth even for a moment, one does not want to return to worldly enjoyment.

Nirvana Upanishad

1. The Soul or Consciousness is beyond the reach of mind and speech.

Shukla Yajur Veda Upanishads.

Adhyatma Upanishad

1. The thought 'I' and 'Mine', the body, the senses and so on, are other than the Self.
2. Dissolve the Self (the mind also called the lower Self with its ego-sense, negative emotions, feelings etc) in the Supreme Self, the Soul as the pot that is destroyed.
3. For the one who has realised the Supreme Soul, there is no transmigration.

Brihad Aranyaka Upanishad

1. The Self is the ruler of all beings. Just as the spokes of a wheel are fixed in the hub of a chariot wheel, so also, all beings, Deities, all worlds and all individual selves are fixed in the Self.

2. The great Self that is birthless resides in the ether or space within the heart. It is the controller and the Lord of all.
3. The Self is immutable and indestructible. The Supreme Consciousness is to be realised through the mind.
4. By knowing the all-pervading Consciousness as oneself, one is not affected by his Karma (that is the thought, word, and deed) as the one who knows it becomes self-restrained, calm, withdrawn and enduring and he sees the all-pervading Consciousness within himself. He also sees all as his very Self. He transcends all evil. He becomes sinless, taintless, and free from all doubts since he has realized the Supreme Truth.

Isavasya Upanishad

1 Performance of one's duties will not bind (entangle) one. The self that is only one, without a second, is faster than the mind; the senses cannot reach it because it goes ahead. It is also stationary but overtakes those who run.

2. The Self moves; yet moves not. It is far as well as near. It is within all and outside all creations.
3. The realised one perceives all beings as his Self and his self as all and therefore he does not entertain hatred towards anything or anyone. What delusion and grief can there be for such a being?
4. The Self that is all-pervading, radiant, bodiless, pure, untainted by sin, is the all-

seeing and all-knowing and also the Lord of the mind, is transcendent and self-contained.

Niralamba Upanishad

1. The Universal Consciousness is the Spirit or Soul. It appears as the ego, the five elements, the macrocosm, the actions, knowledge and so on. It is non-dual and free from all adjuncts. It is all-powerful and is without beginning and end. It is pure, good, the essence of every creation and without qualities.

Paingala Upanishad

1. As there is no difference when water is poured in water, milk in milk, and ghee in ghee, so also there is no difference between the individual Self and the Universal Self.
2. When the mind is transcended, there is no duality of perception. This is the Supreme State of awareness.

Yajna Valkya Upanishad

1. Be convinced that there is Consciousness, that all is Consciousness alone, and is pervaded by Consciousness, that you are Consciousness and I am Consciousness and all the

worlds are also nothing but Consciousness only.

Krisna Yajur Veda Upanishads

Amritha Bindu Upanishad

1. The Universal Self is present in all beings alike. Though one, it is seen as many like the moon in the water.
2. When the mind with its attachment to sense objects is destroyed and is fully restrained, then it realises its essence and the Supreme Self is attained.
3. Realising that one is that immutable consciousness one becomes consciousness
4. The Supreme Consciousness is beyond

reason and analogy, beyond proof and is also causeless. Knowing that the wise becomes ever free.

5. Like butter in milk, pure Consciousness resides in everyone and this should be churned out by the churning rod of the mind.
6. In who resides all beings and who resides in all beings- I am that Soul of the Universe-The Supreme Being.

Brahma Upanishad

The Universe with varied names and forms is held by the Supreme Soul which is the Consciousness, like a collection of gems stringed together on a thread.

1. As the oil is in the sea sum seed, butter in the curd, water in the flowing waves and fire in the wood, so is the soul –the Consciousness to be discovered by one who searches for it, through Truth and Austerity.
2. The Self is the one Lord, self-effulgent, in all beings. As the Self of all beings, it controls and watches over all works both good and bad. It is neither the doer of acts nor its enjoyer. It is the Supreme Intelligence,

the one without a second
and with no attributes

Eakakshara Upanishad

1. consciousness is in all. It is the Lord of the Universe. It is all-knowing, omnipresent and ancient.

2. Consciousness is unthinkable, unmanifest, of innumerable forms, pure, peaceful, immortal, the origin of all creation, without beginning, middle or end, the only one, all-pervading Soul or the Self, permanently blissful, formless and wonderful.
3. Consciousness is all that was, will be, the eternal, immutable, Supreme, and self-luminous. By knowing

Him or That, one transcends death. There is no other way to Freedom.

Katopanishad

1. The self is unborn, eternal, everlasting and ancient. It is not slain when the body is killed.
2. The highest state is wisdom where the five sense organs and mind are at rest and where the intellect is inactive.

Maha Narayana Upanishad

1. All creation abides in the Supreme Consciousness, by whom the entire space is filled, by whom the Sun shines with heat and light, with whom the sages unite

their mind through meditation, by whom the Universe is born, who created the beings with the five elements of Nature, who entered into the beings as their inner Consciousness, who is greater than the greatest, who is one without a second, the imperishable, who is of infinite manifestations, who is ancient, who exists beyond darkness, who is higher than the highest, and subtler than the subtlest and that is imperishable.

2. None can define and limit the nature of Supreme Consciousness.

Sukha Rahasya Upanishad

1. The four major sayings of the Upanishads are,
    a. Consciousness is the Supreme Soul
    b. I am Consciousness
    c. Thou art that Consciousness
    d. The self is Consciousness

Svetasvatara Upanishad

1. The Soul is not male, female or neutral. Whatever body it assumes it becomes identified with that.

Atharva Veda Upanishads

Annapurna Upanishad

When one beholds all beings in one's Self and oneself in all beings, he becomes the Supreme Consciousness.

Almost all these statements about the Soul that are found in the Vedas and Upanishads one can find in Bhagavad Geetha as well.

MARKS OF AN ENLIGHTENED BEING AS TOLD IN BHAGAVAD GEETHA

In chapter -2- verses 55 to 58, chapter 5 from verses 18 to 21, chapter 6 Verses 7 to 9, and Chapter14 from verses 22 to 25, particularly, Lord Krishna explains the characteristic features of a man of wisdom or the enlightened being.

Chapter-2

Verse-55

An enlightened being gives up all cravings of the senses and mind and gets established in his inner Consciousness by himself and becomes blissful always. For such a being worldly pleasures and objects are nothing when compared to this wisdom that ensures freedom from all bondages and sorrows of life and that results in everlasting bliss.

Verse-56.

The sage whose mind is not agitated by the adversities and sorrows of life and whose cravings for worldly pleasures are erased and who is free from all types of attachments, fear and anger is a man of Wisdom.

Verse- 57

He who is unattached to everything around him whether they are good or bad for him and who views all opposites of life as the same by neither rejecting nor rejoicing or getting distressed, when he gets objects that are agreeable or disagreeable to him is a man of stable mind who has attained wisdom.

Verse- 58

When one can withdraw all his senses from sense objects like a tortoise that can withdraw its limbs from all sides, then he is said to have established himself in steady wisdom.

Chapter-5

Verse--18

The sages who have realised the Self have equanimity of vision and they treat everyone and everything equally whether one is a learned one, a cow, an elephant, or a dog.

Verse-19

Those who have such equanimity of vision get liberated from all sorrows and entanglements of life even while living in this world because they are the ones whose mind is steady and well established in the Supreme Soul that is pure, faultless and Absolute.

Verse-20

Such a man who is unperturbed and who has a steady intellect devoid of any delusion has realised the Supreme Reality- the Consciousness. He accepts everything as they come without any preference or prejudice or bias.

Verse 21

Such an enlightened one who is detached from all worldly objects of senses is self-contained and enjoys permanent bliss

Chapter-6

Verse-7

The mind of the realised being is constantly focussed on the Self even amid dualities of life like heat and cold, happiness and sorrow, honour and dishonour, as he is unaffected by these.

Verse-8

The sage who has realised the Self as one who has subjugated his senses treats a lump of earth, or a stone or gold as the same.

Verse-9

The man of spiritual wisdom has equanimity of vision towards one and all whether one is a well-wisher, a friend, a foe, a stranger or an ally, or righteous or unrighteous and hateful or loving.

Chapter14

Verse- 22.

The man of wisdom neither shows aversion towards knowledge that is born out of the quality of goodness, nor the activity that is the product of the quality of Passion or delusion that is of the ignorance when any one of these qualities become dominant in him nor longs for any of these qualities when they are absent.

Such a being always remains unconcerned and remaining as a witness to everything that goes on around him, is not affected or influenced by the experience of the sense objects that are the products of these three qualities. (That means he has transcended all the three qualities of Nature namely goodness, passion and ignorance and has become one who is purity personified.)

Verse -23

The man of Wisdom always remains unconcerned and he remains a mere witness to everything that goes on in the world. He does not get influenced or get affected by the experiences of the sense objects.

Verse- 24

He is well balanced in all dualities of life like pleasure and pain. He finds no difference between a lump of earth, stone or gold. He is the same towards one who hates him or one who loves him and he remains the same when one praises him or blames him.

Verse-25

He treats both honour and humiliation as the same. He views everyone and everything in an equal manner whether one is a friend or foe. He has no sense of ego in whatever he does. He has transcended the three qualities of Nature.

SPIRITUAL PATHS –A BRIEF VIEW

In ancient India, people followed several paths that led to the ultimate Spiritual enlightenment or Wisdom. The various paths enabled one to know the mind, transform the mind from its lower level to the higher level and thereby go beyond the lower emotional mind and reach and experience the higher level of mind that is the same as the Supreme Awareness, or the supreme Universal Consciousness.

The ancient scripture of India particularly Bhagavad Geetha of Lord Krishna gives a detailed account of the four Spiritual paths that a spiritual seeker can follow to experience the ultimate spiritual wisdom. These are Jnana Yoga which is the Path of Knowledge, Karma Yoga which is the path of selfless dedicated service performed with no selfish motive, Bhakti Yoga that is, the path of Devotion and Dhyana Yoga that is the path of Meditation. It also includes Kriya Yoga to a certain extent.

The term Yoga comes from the Sanskrit word 'Yuj' meaning to join or merge or unite or to connect or contact. It also means any spiritual path or technique or method leading to the ultimate goal of Self-Realisation that is, spiritual enlightenment when the individual Soul, merges with the Universal Soul or Consciousness. Sometimes the word also refers to the merging of the mind with our Soul. Patanjali, an ancient Sage of India, in his Ashtanga Yoga means the eight-limbed Yoga defines Yoga as the technique that results in 'Chittha Vruthi Nirodha' that is, the cessation of all modifications of the mind in the form of thoughts. Vruthi in the Sanskrit language, which was the most ancient language which was spoken throughout entire India, refers to the waves or the whirlpool of thoughts and Nirodha means to restrain, control or cessation.

Though the above-mentioned paths seem to be different they are however not contradictory but are complementary to each other and a spiritual seeker can follow any one of these paths or a combination of a few or more paths to reach the spiritual destination. All these paths are also equally important and no single path is either superior or inferior to any other path as the purpose and final goal of all these methods or paths is the same and that is elevating the level of humans by transforming them from being ordinary to becoming extraordinary and from being human to becoming the very Divine-that is the Supreme Intelligence, awareness, spirit, Soul or Consciousness or God the Almighty or whatever we may call it because all these mean the same.

1. The Path of Knowledge - Jnana Marga or Jnana Yoga

In this path the spiritual seeker by acquiring the required spiritual knowledge from his Guru, that is the master who sheds all his ignorance that is like darkness, by bringing in the light of knowledge to him, and by gaining such knowledge from Scriptures and then by remembering, introspecting the knowledge gained, and finally by imbibing and bringing the knowledge to practice, reach the ultimate goal of spiritual wisdom. As this path makes use of the intellect it is called the Path of Knowledge. Jnana means Knowledge and Marga means the path. However, this path is supposed to be comparatively a difficult one because one should have the necessary intelligence to grasp and understand fully the ultimate Spiritual Reality which is abstract, subtle and transcendental. In this path, the effort of the spiritual seeker plays an important role. It is like the baby monkey (the spiritual seeker) holding on to its mother monkey (his Guru or master) tightly so that its mother can carry it wherever she goes.

2. The Path of Selfless Service - Karma Marga or Karma Yoga

One can realise the Supreme Reality also through Selfless, dedicated Service to the entire creation, that is performed wholeheartedly and willingly with no selfish motive either praise or of any type of gain at one time or the other and that which is done in a detached manner and as a dedication to God the Almighty. The Karma Yogi that is, the one who has chosen this path of Selfless Service also performs any service to any of the creations with equanimity of vision that is with a balanced mind. He also serves others without any sense of ego or doer ship. This method is suitable for those who are broadminded, service minded and who can think objectively from the point of view of one and all. In this, the noble thoughts or good emotions in one play an important role.

3. The Path of Devotion - Bhakthi Marga or Bhakthi Yoga

In the Path of Devotion, one connects oneself with the formless ultimate Consciousness that is beyond any form, or limitation, through Deities with forms. The Deities installed in the Temple are energised through several techniques known as Tantras, Mantras and Yantras and so on. This path is best suited for a devotee who is completely devoted to God with total unconditional love, faith and surrender to the Almighty. Just as the mother cat carries its kitten with no effort on the part of the kitten but by the efforts of the mother cat alone, similarly the devotee in this path feels no responsibility for all that is happening in his life because of his full trust in God that makes him surrender himself at the feet of God in an unconditional manner. A real devotee does not seek anything from God because he is fully aware that God knows and does only what is to be done for the devotee and the devotee accepts what comes in his life with an open mind without any questioning and without analysing why it is so for him because he knows that God, the creator and who sustains the entire creation including him knows what is best for the devotee. So even when adverse things happen in his life, he does not get shattered. He humbly accepts everything as the will of God. This path though looks very simple, is not easy for all because one has to be extremely humble and egoless and full of love towards God. Generally, although most of us have faith in God still it is only conditional. We don't spare even God when we face any misfortune in life and we usually ask 'Why me' of all the people God chose for such a happening and whenever we are blessed with anything in life, we feel that it is due to our efforts and brain power and most of our prayers are only seeking something or the other from God.

4. The Path of Meditation- Dhyana Marga or Dhyana Yoga.

The term Dhyana_comes from the Sanskrit term Dhai which_means to 'think of'. The method used in this path is the one-pointed attention on a particular single object or thought, which can be a place, person, God, concept, mantra, idol and so on. However, it is not concentration. This is because Meditation or Dhyana has to be practised in a calm and relaxed manner without one being tense, then only it will yield the desired result. In this method, one's mind needs to be watchful without getting diverted. However, as we know at least at the beginning of meditation no one can eliminate all thoughts except the one on which he is supposed to focus upon. So, it is advised that one should try to gradually reduce the number of his thoughts during the beginning stages of meditation. This must be done in a relaxed manner. As soon as one realises that his mind is getting diverted and as soon as he becomes aware that other thoughts are entering into his mind then, realising that, one should bring back his mind to the one single thought that he focuses upon. This should not be done in a forceful manner but in a very friendly and, understanding manner. He should also at the same time, bring the mind back to the thought that he focuses upon. While answering the question put by Arjuna regarding the wandering nature of the mind that is like that of a monkey that always jumps from one branch to another branch of the tree, and how to control the very nature of the mind that always has a continuous flow of thoughts Lord Krishna replies that what Arjuna has said is true but one can surely, without any doubt can make the mind to focus on one single thought in course of time after a regular, and prolonged meditation that is practised in an earnest and committed manner and that it is not impossible but always possible for all humans. When the spiritual seeker goes on practising any meditation technique in this manner then gradually, it is said by the enlightened ones, that a time will come when thoughts start disappearing gradually and naturally, and finally that single thought on which one focuses also will vanish and that is the stage when there is no mind because the mind can exist only when there are thoughts. When all thoughts are dead mind also ceases. And only the Self that merges with the Universal self remains, which means that the mind, not as thoughts but in its purest form as the Soul will remain but nothing else. It is like butter, when heated getting transformed into ghee finally when all the impurities that were in the butter get lost then, only the pure ghee remains. Once this happens then one realises or becomes Conscious of the fact that the Soul in him is only a part of the true reflection of the Universal Soul and all-pervading that is the Universal Consciousness. And at that point, he becomes a Realised being or an Enlightened being. He becomes the same as the Universal Consciousness by losing all his separate identity. It is like a lump of salt dissolving in the ocean by merging with the water in the ocean. He then becomes a pure being, a man of wisdom who becomes the same as the transcendental Universal Consciousness.

All the above-mentioned spiritual paths may look different from each other outwardly, but they are not however contradictory to each other but are very much complementary. For example, all the paths, irrespective of the fact whether it is the path of Knowledge, Service, or devotion require one-pointed attention or focus whether it is Dhyana or Meditation, knowledge, service, or devotion. Similarly, one has to obtain the necessary knowledge to follow any of these paths. Again, like a true devotee, one must be humble enough without ego and should have total faith and trust in the master and in the path that he chooses to follow. One can choose any one of the paths or even a combination of more than one path depending upon his aptitude and inherent nature.

A few techniques followed in religious and spiritual practices in India

One can also come across very many techniques or means or tools that are being made use of for spiritual and religious practises in India since ancient times. Some of these are,

1. Tantra

Tantra means loom, weave or warp. It is an ancient technique, method or path, or even a text that is broadly applicable or a system. In some scriptures, it is also defined as a doctrine, a kind of technique of worship. Both in Hinduism and Buddhism, one can see the use of Tantras. Kashmir Shaivism makes use of this method. In Hindu Temples, the Tantra technique is mostly used in

Temple construction. Tantras also make use of physical diagrams that are mathematically precise and Mantras are specific sounds that produce vibrations in space. Those who practise this technique are usually called Tantrics. Various physical postures or diagrams and gestures and movements of hands are used in this to transform one to a higher dimension. One can see on the outer walls of the temple many erotic sex postures that are depicted. This has given rise to many derogatory remarks by some against Tantra. But if one goes deeper into its meaning then one will only be aghast at the way the ancient Indians understood the basic instincts and psychology of human beings as in any other creation. The different sex poses are depicted on the walls of the temple because it is understood by the ancients that one who enters into the

Temple at least for the time being when he comes to worship the Deity to elevate himself spiritually through the path of Devotion, should go beyond the feeling of sex, that is one of the fundamental urges in any adult being, starting from the lowest to the highest species of creation. The devotee who enters the Temple first of all comes across these artistic paintings, drawings or carvings and so on, at the outer Temple wall and his attention is automatically drawn towards those and he starts looking at these. These attract him automatically and he goes on viewing the various postures of sex all around the Temple wall while he performs circumambulation around the Temple. As he goes on looking at such paintings, drawings or carvings that are innumerable, he gradually starts losing interest in these and by the time he comes to the entrance of the Temple to get into the Temple, he would have completely become a transformed man at least for the time being by becoming indifferent to all his sexual feelings. It is similar to that of a cook who cooks a variety of dishes and items and after cooking the dishes, loses interest in the food that he cooked. He may even dislike the very odour of the ingredients that he used for the cooking and he may even refuse to taste the dishes and the items that he had cooked. This is because the continuous association of the cook for a significantly long time with those made him averse to the very food that he had prepared nicely and in a careful manner. It is so for the entire creation. When any creature or being is given more and more of something that he craves until then, still, a time will come when he will start rejecting them because he is more than satiated with that and a stage will come when he will want no more of it and he may even start disliking it and finally, he turns away from it. This psychology of beings is made use of here. It is also because sex, which is considered proper, is what is accepted by the norms of any society and is not taboo in Hinduism. By the time one enters into the sanctum sanctorum, the devotee will have no such thoughts in his mind except that of the Deity.

2. Mantra

Mantras are sacred syllables, words or a set of words or prayers or sacred formulae, the utterance of which produces sounds and powerful vibrations in the atmosphere. The Mantras are uttered either internally that is silently within oneself or loudly. They are repeated several times When it is uttered loudly or internally. It is understood that they produce some vibrations in space and the sound vibrations are used to spiritually elevate one to the level of the Supreme Consciousness. Mantras also form an important part of prayers and rituals performed in the worship of Deities and also in Meditation. In this, the mind is made to focus on the Mantras that are uttered. Repeated Mantra chanting is supposed to develop one's mental powers and strength, ease tensions and stress and elevate one to the highest level of Consciousness. Sometimes the Mantras are also inscribed on the Yantras.

3. Yantra

Yantra means an instrument, machine or talisman and is a physical energy diagram that is mystical and geometrical and with different shapes like triangles, squares, circles and so on, that are supposed to represent the energy fields of specific Deities by meditating on which one can become spiritually enlightened. Yantra means a tool that helps one to restrain one's mind. In Hinduism, there are specific Yantras associated with specific Deities.

A few other types of Spiritual practises in India since ancient times.

There are also a few other types of Yogas and spiritual practices that are supposed to be followed with expert guidance only. These are,

1. Hata Yoga

Hata Yoga is also an ancient Indian technique of Yoga. In this Yoga or the spiritual path or technique, the Yogi tries to bring balance between the Sun and the Moon within his body, which is represented by the two important central subtle Nadis namely the Ida and Pingala Nadis that are subtle energy channels and that represent the masculine and feminine energies within the body. In this one manipulates the energy system and moves the system in a certain manner through various very difficult physical postures and drives the energy within in a specific direction. In this Yoga technique, it is said that there are 84 fundamental postures. Hata also literally means 'force'. This technique is based upon various physical postures like twisting of the body where certain force needs to be applied. That may also be the reason why it is called Hata Yoga. This technique is very powerful and has to be practised only with expert guidance, otherwise, it will result in harmful results.

2. Sage Patanjali's eight-limbed Yoga-The Ashtanga Yoga

Patanjali was one of the many ancient sages that India has witnessed. Of all the books that he wrote, the book on Yoga Soothras is considered the greatest. This book is supposed to have been written by Patanjali around the second B C E. The Yoga Soothras is a classical yoga text. His Yoga Soothras is supposed to contain 196 Soothras or aphorisms on the theory and practise of Yoga. Soothra means a string that holds beads or any set of sacred words in order or the principles that hold certain things in order. Patanjali's Yoga Soothras include not only the actual practice of Meditation but also contains the eight steps that he calls the eight limbs of his Yoga that one should observe for practising meditation.

The eight limbs of Patanjali's yoga are namely, 1. Yama or external discipline or ethical standards or code of conduct. 2. Niyama or internal discipline 3. Asanas or Yoga postures 4. Pranayama or restraining the flow of breath 5. Pratyahara or withdrawal of sensory ability of organs 6. Dharana uninterrupted Focus 7. Dhyana or high level of Meditation and 8. Samadhi is absorption into the infinite- the Chittha that is Consciousness.

1. There are five Yamas. These are A. Ahimsa or non-violence concerning the entire creation B. Satya or Truthfulness Telling the Truth only and if this is not possible, then, at least maintaining silence, C. Asteya, non-stealing, that is, refraining oneself from stealing any type of property that belongs to some other person. D. Aparigraha or Non- coveting that is not being greedy and not

becoming jealous or enviable of other's possessions and E. Brahmacharya or celibacy or sexual restraint while one is a student in the process of learning as his entire attention should be focussed on learning. These are the five moral principles which are the basis of the right code of conduct that one should follow.

2. Niyamas relate to the internal disciplines that are to be practised. There are five Niyamas. These are A. Sauucha or cleanliness. This is related to the purification of both body as well as the mind B. Santosha or contentment or genuine happiness with whatever one has, without craving for more and more. C. Tapas, which is generally known as Dhyana or Meditation. Although Meditation is an important aspect here, Tapas includes not only Meditation or Dhyana but also several other spiritual

austerities like persistence, perseverance, and prayer, that are to be practised by the Yogi physically and mentally. D. Svadhyaya or the study of scriptures about one's Self. After the student who is called Brahmachari acquires the required knowledge, then, he is supposed to introspect that knowledge in his mind, and memorize by repeatedly uttering the knowledge that is usually in the form of Mantras, Prayers etc. and analyse his thoughts, words and deeds and practise Eshwara Pranidhana or contemplation on God as the ultimate Supreme Reality- The Universal Consciousness with total surrender, faith and Trust.

3. Asanas relate to the various postures of the body that are steady, comfortable, motionless and relaxed. In its original sense, Asana means only a comfortable seat. In the Yoga of Patanjali Asanas

refer to the various postures of the body that are either simple or complex that promote physical health and mental well-being. Asanas can be in sitting posture or standing or reclining, backward bending, forward bending and soon.

4. Pranayama is restraining the movement of breath in a particular manner. Prana means the vital breath and Yama means discipline. Pranayama is done in many ways. One can find many breathing techniques in this like breathing through one nostril and letting it out through the other nostril, suspending breathing for a short duration of time, slowing down the breathing process, consciously changing the length of breath through deep breathing or fast breathing, inhaling and exhaling breath through the same nostril and soon. Pranayama helps in reducing

thoughts or arresting the flow of thoughts and thereby brings inward calmness.

5. Pratyahara is the withdrawal of senses that are always outward bound. It helps one to move away from external things and move towards the interior. By shutting the doors of the mind that activates the senses, the mind can be turned inward and reach the core of the heart wherein is the Spirit and finally can become one with the Spirit or Soul.

6. Dharana is focussing. It refers to the inner journey of the mind through focus or contemplation or uninterrupted watchfulness or total attention towards the object of meditation. It is one-pointedness of mind.

7. Dhyana or Meditation. This is supposed to be the ultimate stage of Meditation. In this one focuses upon a

particular object only by excluding all other thoughts so that, that single thought only will remain and after some time that single thought also will disappear and finally one reaches the ultimate state of enlightenment.

8. Samadhi or State of equanimity or Spiritual enlightenment. When one can synchronise Pratyahara, Dharana and Dhyana then one reaches the final stage of Samadhi. This is the stage- the point of the merger when the Yogi ultimately transcends himself and reaches the highest state of Consciousness that is, the state of Enlightenment-ecstasy or Blissfulness.

3. Kundalini Yoga

The term Kundalini comes from the Sanskrit word 'Kundal' which means circular. It also refers to a coiled snake. Kundalini is supposed to represent the feminine spiritual energy in our bodies. It is an important concept in Shaiva Tantra. It is understood that this concept is found even in the Vedic texts. As such it is an ancient technique of Yoga. It uses chanting of Mantras for directing the coiled-up energy that is roused. In this Yoga, one focuses and observes the movement of breath and creates a feeling that the energy is moving up along the spine. In this practice along with meditation Pranayama (Breath-control), Asanas (the physical postures), Tantras, Yantras and Mantras are also used.

In Kundalini Yoga Kundalini represents the subtle coiled-up feminine dormant energy at the base of the spin. Symbolically it is represented as a serpent that is coiled three and a half times within us at the base of the Spine where the Mooladhara Chakra or the root Chakra is considered the subtle wheel of energy, is located. When the Kundalini that is the coiled-up energy is roused or activated through meditation then it moves up with great speed along the spine through the seven subtle wheels of energy called the Chakras and finally reaches the Crown Chakra which is known as the Sahasrara Chakra and then one gets spiritual enlightenment. It is the state of an expanded state of Consciousness. This Yoga also results in physical and mental well-being. The Kundalini experience, that is when Kundalini rises one is supposed to get a clear feeling of electric current running along the spine that is called Meru Danda.

In his book on Raja Yoga, Swami Vivekananda describes his ultimate experience of Kundalini awakening. He says as the Kundalini shoots up layer after layer and then, the mind becomes open and all the different visions and wonderful powers come to the Yogi, that is, the one who practises the Yoga and one finally experiences an expanded state of Consciousness. This Yoga is also called the 'Yoga of Awareness'.

However, this yoga is very powerful and therefore very dangerous. This should be practised only directly under the proper guidance of an expert in this Yoga. It should be handled in a very efficient manner and correct manner. It may lead to undesirable and dangerous consequences if it is practised incorrectly. This practice is mostly meant for ascetics.

4. Chakra Meditation or Meditation on the wheels of Energy

Chakra Meditation is similar to Kundalini Meditation. In Chakra

Meditation, one activates the Chakras that are supposed to be the wheels of energy in our body. In Kundalini yoga, the Yogi activates the Kundalini energy which is supposed to be the subtle spiritual feminine energy located at the base of the spine, specifically in the root Chakra that is known as the Mooladhara Chakra. When it is roused, it shoots up along the Chakras activating them in the process and finally reaches the Sahasrara Chakra or the Crown Chaka. At this when one experiences enlightenment.

Chakra in Sanskrit means subtle wheels or cycles of energy in our body. It also means disc. These are whirling or spinning energy centres in our bodies. The seven main Chakras run through the spine from its bottom up to the top of the head. These are supposed to be the locations where our life energy or Prana concentrate. It is also understood that there are 109 Chakras in our body. Some say that there are 12 Chakras. This is the number found in one of the Meditation techniques given by Lord Shiva Himself. However, Chakra Meditation is concerned only with the most important seven Chakras that are within our body.

The seven important Chakras, the emotions that are related to them, their colour and the element associated with them are,

1. The Mooladhara Chakra or the Root Chakra is located at the base of the spine that is in the Mooladhara or the root or the Sacrum. It is connected with the mental stability of one. It governs the way we conduct ourselves with the outside world. It also governs

our basic needs like food and shelter. It is associated with the red colour and the element of earth.

2. Swadishtana Chakra is located behind the genitals that are below the navel. It is linked to sex and the creative process and creative abilities in one. Its colour is orange and the element is water.
3. Manipooraka, that is, in the solar plexus region, that is the navel region and is known as the mid-brain region. It regulates our emotions and desires. It is also the source of self-esteem and digestive function. Its colour is yellow and is associated with the fire element.
4. Anahata Chakra or Heart Chakra is located at the region of the chest in the heart and lung region. Anahata in Sanskrit means 'unstuck'. It is associated with noble emotions

like unconditional love, generosity, the ability to appreciate, compassion, and inclusiveness to mention a few. It is green in colour and the element is air.

5. Visuddhi Chakra or the throat Chakra is located at the base of the throat. It is associated with communication, confidence and understanding. Its colour is blue and its element is the sky that is space or ether.
6. Ajna Chakra also referred to as the Third Eye of Lord Shiva, is located at the centre of the two eyebrows. This chakra enables one to figure out many things mentally, emotionally and also spiritually. It governs the spiritual intuition and insight in one. A well-balanced activated Ajna Chakra empowers one to know about the world and

also beyond it. Its colour is indigo and its element is light.

7. Sahasrara Chakra or the Crown Chakra is located 2” above the top of the head. It is supposed to radiate upward.t is also referred to as the Lotus with thousand petals. This Chakra is considered the most spiritual Chakra. This Chakra helps us in our spiritual awakening or enlightenment. Its colour is purple/violet and it embodies the Soul within us.

All seven Chakras process and distribute the necessary energy required for our health and well-being. When the Chakras are opened up, that is, activated, then energy effortlessly flows throughout the body. On the contrary when the Chakras are dormant then they will block the energy flow and will bring about an imbalance in the body, mind and spirit.

When the Chakras are activated, one gets immense energy and the associated emotions will also be enhanced. All positive qualities in one will become more pronounced and his negative tendencies will disappear. Chakra Meditation will make the body and mind more balanced, relaxed and calm. More than everything this will lead to spiritual Enlightenment

The Chakra Meditation should be practised only under the direct guidance and supervision of a master who is an expert in this Yoga. Otherwise, it will lead to many adverse results that are dangerous and harmful to one.

5. Kriya Yoga

In a very broad sense, Kriya Yoga is a technique in which the energy in our body is controlled through Pranayama which can be broadly understood as breath control and meditation that quickens the spiritual process, ultimately resulting in spiritual enlightenment. Kriya means action. This is considered an ancient yoga practice that had disappeared long ago for several centuries. It was later revived in 1861 by Mahavir Babaji and later passed on through his disciple Lahiri Mahasaya.

In Kriya Yoga, the Prana or the life energy is directed upward and downward around the Chakras which are called the wheels of energy located invisibly along the spinal column. This is a physiological technique. Lord Krishna mentioned this technique in his Bhagavad Geetha in chapter 4, verse 29 wherein he says that those who practise Pranayama regulate the movement of Prana, that is, the upward movement of the vital energy and Apana that is the downward movement of the vital energy. They offer Prana (inhaling breath) into the Apana (exhaling breath) and offer Apana (the exhaling breath) into Prana (the inhaling breath) during Vedic Sacrifices that are known as Yagas and Yagnas in the Sanskrit language. In this way, the Yogi neutralises these two Pranas-the-life currents and this results from mutation of decay and growth of the physical body. It is also said that the Yoga Soothras of Sage Patanjali also contain a description of Kriya Yoga in the second chapter where it is stated that the Ultimate permanent Liberation or Freedom one can obtain by that Pranayama, or breath control in the broad sense, that is accompanied by disjoining the course of inspiration and expiration. In this, a Mantra or a word is used to focus one's attention which will enable him to go deep into meditation.

How to practise Meditation or Dhyana

Before starting Meditation, one should observe the following

1. Select a quiet place for meditation.
2. Sit in a comfortable position.
3. Sit in a very relaxed manner and without moving your body because body movement will lead to distraction of the mind.
4. Sit in an erect position so that your spinal column is straight. This will make the subtle energy pass through from the bottom to the top of your head very quickly.

5. Close your eyes except in those meditation techniques that are done with open eyes.
6. Do not move your eyelids. This is likely to distract your attention.
7. Spend some time settling down and then only start focussing.
8. Practise meditation continuously without any considerable break unless when one becomes unwell because any break continuously for days or weeks or months will slow down the pace with which you can progress. However, when one is unwell, he can resume his meditation after he gets well.
9. One should focus his attention, become watchful and contemplate upon the object of his meditation in a very relaxed

casual manner. But one should not concentrate on the object. This will result in headaches and heaviness in the head.

10. Meditation that is focus or watchfulness or total attention or contemplation can be on any particular thought, object, place, breath or parts of the body or God or anything. Visualise in your mind that upon which you are meditating.

11. The object of meditation is not important. One is supposed to choose an object for meditation because it becomes impossible for an ordinary being to focus his attention otherwise. It is beyond the capacity of ordinary human beings to focus their attention on formless Universal Energy or Consciousness. Hence the need

for an object for focusing one’s attention whether it is a place, a thing, a person or even God and so on.

12. Do not be in a hurry to reach the destination and enjoy the benefits of meditation. It is a long process. The mind is like a monkey's. It will wander from one thought to another thought very quickly. It is also not easy to bring back the mind and make it focus constantly on the object of meditation. It needs constant, prolonged, continuous and persistent meditation.
13. In the initial stages whenever your mind gets diverted to other thoughts, every time bring back the mind to the object of your meditation in a friendly, understanding manner by

gracefully removing all other thoughts from your mind. Gradually you will be able to reduce and even eliminate all other thoughts and focus only on the object of your meditation in an uninterrupted manner that is when the mind starts calming and settling down. Osho says that in meditation one should start observing all thoughts that come to one in an impartial, non-judgmental manner without evaluation, favour or disfavour, without forming any conclusions, merely as a witness or observer as though he is watching a procession that is passing on.

14. Do not bring back the mind from other thoughts forcefully.

15. To start with remain in that position and try your best to focus only on the object of meditation at least for 20 minutes. Gradually try to increase the duration, that is, the time allotted for meditation. Then in course of time, it will not be difficult for one to become meditative always whatever he may be doing. It is also preferable to meditate at the same time and in the same plays every day. Usually, the twilight period during both morning and evening is considered to be the best time for meditation. These are called the Sandhyas or the junction points between day and night and night and day. However, one can also meditate whenever he gets time, for

example, as soon as he gets up from bed in the morning or when he goes to bed at night and so on. Automatically one will be able to meditate for a longer duration of time that is when one starts enjoying the benefits of meditation. When you become meditative always that is, all the time, then the duration of time, place etc. becomes irrelevant because at that stage one becomes meditative always. Later, gradually, after some time, you will see only yourself and the object of your meditation, that is, the one who sees the object mentally who is the subject or the observer and the object of meditation that is the seen or observed.

16. After some time, you will realise that the distance between the observer and the observed, that is, between the subject and the object starts decreasing gradually.
17. Then at one point in time, without any of your effort, all of a sudden, even without your awareness you will suddenly get awakened and you become a different person. At that point, you will start experiencing that there is nothing else except the subject or the observer, that is, your Self that is called the Jeevatman (the individual Soul or Spirit) in the Sanskrit language, because the object then gets dissolved in the subject. This is the stage when you realise the ultimate Truth that was there already. That means you are

not discovering or inventing anything new because what you realise at the final stage was already there even before, but about which you were till then completely ignorant. At such a point you will become aware of the fact that everything is only the Self in you, that is also the Universal all-pervading Self or Consciousness but nothing else and this awareness leads to freedom from all bondages, sufferings and pains of life. This is the ultimate state when one forgets himself and starts enjoying and becoming the permanent Bliss, Joy or Ananda.

Without any doubt in the initial stages, one finds meditation very difficult. It becomes impossible to sit for a considerable time with focus on a single thought. When such a one determines to fix his thought on the object of his meditation, even without his own knowing many other thoughts will start coming and crowding his mind. It may also be difficult for him to sit for the meditation at a specific time and in a specific place. Over and above everything he is not sure when he will start getting the benefits from meditation. It also requires long, continuous, persistent effort, patience, total faith, trust and surrender. But despite all these hurdles if one determines to continue practising meditation then after some time it will automatically become easy, effortless and interesting for him especially when he starts witnessing the good and positive changes in his thoughts, words and actions that will eventually bring a lot of happiness and peace within himself and also for the others around him.

Benefits of Dhyana Yoga or Meditation

Dhyana or Meditation is a very powerful tool not only for spiritual enlightenment but also for good physical health and mental well-being. Spiritually it makes one go beyond his body and mind and culminates in spiritual wisdom or enlightenment that makes one, who was till then very ordinary into an extraordinary human being with several astonishing powers. His very presence will make others good human beings and become happy and peaceful. Much scientific research also has proved that Meditation in its course brings about physical health and mental well-being to the meditator. When such men of spiritual wisdom outnumber the other ordinary people then, without any doubt the whole world will become a heaven where there will be global peace and harmony without any ill will or hatred against each other.

Physical health benefits

Physically it brings about overall better health, improves the quality of sleep, gives better cardiac health, increases brain power, reduces medication, and prevents colds, flu, headache, gastrointestinal disorders, diabetes, hypertension, heart diseases, allergies, asthma, and other chronic ailments.

Mental wellbeing

In addition to this meditation eliminates mental and psychological problems like depression, and anxiety, brings about greater inner peace, emotional balance, greater capacity to concentrate and focus, greater clarity, increased energy levels, increases self-confidence, productivity in work, improves intuitive ability, mental alertness, self-awareness and so on. Meditation also increases intuition and creativity.

Spiritual Wisdom

When one becomes spiritually enlightened then he becomes the happiest and the most peaceful person in the world who enjoys total and permanent Freedom from all the pains and sufferings of worldly life. He becomes fearless and a good human being with all positivity in his mind. There will not be any trace of negativity in him. His positive outlook and nature and goodness enhance his Aura- the spiritual energy, in him and people will get attracted towards him. He also enjoys unimaginable powers that he uses for the welfare of the entire creation irrespective of the level of creation, that is whether they are immovable or movable. The benefits extend even to those around him because, such a person spreads happiness, peace, goodness and so on to one and all. He can also bring about a remarkable change in the mindset of the people for good. By being a model for others he can bring a transformation in the thought process, words and actions of others. For example, the one who was full of negativity in his mind will start becoming a better human being and will start exhibiting more and more positive qualities that will benefit him as well as others.

PART---2

THE MEDITATION TECHNIQUES OF LORD SHIVA

It is said that Lord Shiva himself, in the beginning, imparted the knowledge of meditation to mankind through His consort, Goddess Parvathi. In the process, Lord Shiva is supposed to have given several meditation techniques for mankind to follow for attaining Spiritual Wisdom. It is also told that these techniques were given by Lord Shiva as answers to all the queries that were put by Goddess Parvathi to Lord Shiva for clearing her doubts regarding Spirituality.

It is believed that once during their intimate moments Goddess Parvathi said to Lord Shiva,

"OH, My Lord, although I have learnt all about Creation, still, I have certain doubts that I need to clarify from you. Kindly be gracious to impart the necessary knowledge to clear all my doubts".

In essence, the questions of Goddess Parvathi related to,

What are the real form and real nature of the Almighty -Lord Shiva, how can one know Him and attain Him and become the same as the Lord The Almighty, the all-pervading Universal Soul?

Lord Shiva was very much pleased with the Goddess for asking such questions and therefore, He said,

"Oh, my dear, you have asked excellent questions that are nothing but the essence and the secrets of Tantra. Even though the subject is very difficult to grasp, still, I shall explain the knowledge about that to you".

After uttering these words Lord Shiva started to clear the doubts expressed by

His Consort and began to answer the questions put by Her.

(A brief account of what the Lord stated)

Lord Shiva said, that all the various forms of God are not a reality. The God or the Almighty has no form. The different forms of God are only to help the ordinary people who are not spiritually elevated and therefore are unable to fix their attention on the Almighty-the Universal Consciousness, that is without any form.

People also think that God- the Almighty is different from them. They are not aware of the fact that the same Universal energy, the power, the Consciousness, the Almighty, the Soul, is present within their body as the individual soul or the individual Consciousness. God, in reality, therefore is not a form, sound or anything.

The Nature of God is such that He is beyond time and direction. He is unlimited, vast, expansive, pure, perfect, omnipotent, omniscient and omnipresent. The state of God can never be measured by time, space or direction. It cannot even be indicated through any attribute or description.

God the Supreme is within each one of the entire creations as the individual Soul that in the Sanskrit language is known as the Jeevaatman. The individual Soul is only a part or the true reflection of God within each one of the entire creations. The Supreme, the Universal Consciousness that is God, is unlimited, pure joy, all-pervading and so on, so also each Soul in each of the creations. However, due to ignorance, beings imagine that they are different from God. This is because they identify themselves with their body and mind are perishable and therefore are only temporary. Only through Spiritual discipline and practice of Spiritual techniques or methods the beings will realise that they are the same as God, the Almighty Himself or itself.

It is impossible to explain and describe God as words or languages have limitations. One has to experience God by himself. For that one has to go through a long and, prolonged arduous, honest and committed spiritual process and practice. Then only one can know and realise God and His Nature.

Only when a person goes beyond his mind, that is, when all his thoughts stop, and when the mind becomes still without thoughts then it will automatically merge into what is called the Universal Consciousness and will become that Universal Soul or Consciousness. That is the stage when he experiences God within himself and enjoys infinite joy which is known as Bliss that is immeasurable, infinite, and everlasting. Such an inner experience of Joy one obtains only when he gets freed from all thoughts. The one who experiences such joy will never, again, turn towards worldly pleasures and enjoyments of life because when compared to the infinite bliss that he enjoys the worldly pleasures look so trivial to him and he never cares for such pleasures of life.

All the spiritual practises that one has to go through for achieving the above-mentioned goal of permanent Bliss require one-pointedness of mind that can be obtained through meditation, because, only meditation can subjugate the mind and make it turn inwards that is usually turned outward seeking worldly enjoyments of life that can never bring eternal peace and happiness. The mind also jumps from one thought to another in a ceaseless manner and this results in restlessness of the mind. Meditation helps one to reduce the number of thoughts in the beginning and finally, it enables one to go beyond the mind by the cessation of all thoughts and when there are no thoughts then there is no mind either. This is because the mind can exist only when there are thoughts. Thoughts are the basis of the mind, so, when the foundation or the base itself collapses the whole structure, in this case, the mind also collapses without any trace whatsoever. At this stage, the mind disappears totally because it has merged with the Universal existence.

This is the stage when one realises and experiences God and he becomes God by merging with that- the spirit or Soul or the Universal energy.

In reality God the Almighty, the Universal Soul is neither male nor female. God and the Goddess are the same. The creative aspect of energy is the Goddess. Just as the burning power of fire cannot be different from fire because the power of burning is inherent in fire, similarly, there can be no difference between energy and the possessor of the energy. They are the same. However, Shiva and Shakthi (Parvathi) are imagined to be separate in the beginning stages of spirituality, as a preliminary step in spiritual knowledge, for elevating oneself spiritually after a certain stage in the spiritual process. The Goddess (Parvathi) is the entrance to God (Lord Shiva). So, when one enters into the state of Divine energy, (the Goddess) then, one is in the state of God as well. Just as through the rays of the sun or by any means of light, space, direction, form etc, are revealed, similarly, through the medium of the Divine energy that is, the Goddess, the all-pervading Space that is the Universal Soul or Consciousness can be realised. That is, God can be realised.

After listening to Lord Shiva very attentively, the Goddess finally asked Her Lord, as to the ways and means by which one can attain the state of the Supreme, that is, realise God and Lord Shiva then began to give the various techniques of meditation through which one can realise the Supreme Energy or the Universal Consciousness.

It is said, that one who earnestly, with faith, follows even any one of these methods of meditation imparted by Lord Shiva is bound to become a Spiritually advanced and enlightened Soul.

The above-mentioned conversation between Lord Shiva and Goddess Parvathi one can find in the book namely, Vigyan Bhairava Tantra, which belongs to a particular form of Yoga called Kashmiri Shaivism that is based upon the philosophy of non-dualism or Monism that is also known as Advaita Vedanta in the ancient Indian Philosophical doctrines. This text is a part of Rudramala Tantra and it is understood that this text is mostly lost and only a few of its parts are available now.

According to Advaita Vedanta, the entire creation is only a part of God. – That is, a part of the Universal Soul or Energy. The Universal Soul is present in every creation, whether it is animate or inanimate, in the form of an individual Soul or Consciousness. Hence there is no difference between God and the entire creation. The difference lies in the fact that while creation has limitations, God is unbounded. While the creation exhibits imperfections due to their body-mind consciousness, and therefore are not pure, God is purity personified. But if one through persistent efforts tries to reach, realise and become the very God then he becomes the Vast, boundless, expansive Consciousness that we call God or the Universal Soul or Energy or the Supreme most power that is the source, the maintainer and also the destroyer who destroys everything for starting a new beginning or a new cycle of the creation process, meant for the upkeep of the endless cyclical process of repeated creation, upkeep, and destruction. Once a person gets the necessary Spiritual Wisdom, he, then, goes beyond his body-mind consciousness with the realisation that in reality, he is not his body or mind which are his accessories and instruments that help in his worldly life, and also in achieving the necessary spiritual Wisdom, but more importantly, the Soul that is a part of the Almighty- The vast, expansive, all-pervading Consciousness, Awareness or Soul and this realisation of the reality makes him Soul Conscious. That is, he will realise his true identity, as the very Soul that is enclosed in the body and that is a part of the all-pervading Consciousness.

It is believed that this book 'Vigyan Bhairava Tntra' is more than 2000 years old and this was supposed to have been written by an unknown author. It is said that this text in its original form is lost now and is not available. This book is titled ‘Vigyan Bhairava Tantra’. Vigyan in the Sanskrit language means ‘Wisdom’, ‘Bhairava’ refers to God, particularly a form of Lord Shiva, and Tantra refers to a certain type of technique of Yoga about which a brief idea is already given in the first section. ‘Rava’ in Sanskrit means Sound and ‘Bhairava’ means that which is beyond sound- that is, Lord Shiva, the Universal Energy.

The discourse between Lord Shiva and Goddess Parvathi is given in this book in 163 Sanskrit Anustubh (a metrical unit found in Vedic and classical Sanskrit poetry) stanzas.

THE MEDITATION TECHNIQUES IMPARTED BY LORD SHIVA

Only the one who is spiritually inclined and has some background in this field will be able to understand the meditation techniques as they can be fully understood only by a spiritual master who can impart not only the required knowledge but also can practically make the disciple practise the techniques. More than anything, the Spiritual Truth has to be experienced by one. Mere knowledge of Spiritual Truth cannot take anyone anywhere. It is futile. One has to experience it by Himself and for that only practical application is the way out.

Another important aspect that we have to notice in the following meditation techniques of Lord Shiva is that it is the fixing of one's attention, but not the object of meditation that is the most important. Lord Shiva himself mentions several objects upon which one may meditate, including one's breath, parts of the body, a place, any single activity, the vast vacant Space and so on. This is because the very objective and final goal of meditation is the realisation of God, and this is possible only when one goes beyond his mind by becoming thoughtless. It is for this purpose alone, that some object is chosen so that one can fix one's attention on that single object because then his mind will think only of that object but nothing else. (The nature of the mind is such that, usually, innumerable thoughts appear and disappear in the mind very quickly, and in a ceaseless manner.) Gradually even that single thought will disappear from his mind and this is the juncture when one goes beyond the mind because there is nothing called the mind for such a person at that moment because for the mind to survive and exist thoughts are necessary. When all thoughts vanish then there is no mind either.

LORD SHIVA'S TECHNIQUES OF MEDITATION

1. Fix the mind at the two points or places from where the incoming and the outgoing breath starts or originates. The vital energy goes upwards and downwards as a result of inhalation and exhalation. One may concentrate on the starting point of both the incoming and outgoing breaths. Continuous contemplation in this manner will enable the spiritual aspirant to realise the Supreme, omnipotent power-the Almighty.

2. Similarly, one may restrain both the incoming and the outgoing breaths at the

junction points of their return. That is, one should go on observing the two junction points where the breath turns from outside to inside and from inside to outside. When one focuses on the turning points of the two breaths, then, the mind becomes focused on the present breathing activity only and gradually it will stop functioning altogether without any trace. At this point the true nature of God, the Almighty will be revealed to one after such prolonged meditation.

3. Retain the breath inside, as long as it is possible so that the breathing is still without any movement. This is the centre where the breath neither goes in nor goes out. When one observes this, after a prolonged meditation, the gap between the incoming and outgoing breaths then, all thoughts will start disappearing that is, the mind will be

without thoughts and it will disappear. Then, one attains the state of the Almighty.

4. When the breath after prolonged meditation, stops by itself for some time, that is, automatically gets retained inside after inhalation or exhalation then, by experiencing the inner energy only (Goddess Parvathi or Shakthi), the state of God- The Consciousness is revealed.

In all the four above-mentioned breathing techniques, the breath is focussed upon and one starts observing the gap in the breathing, then, slowly and gradually the breathing slows down and the gap between the incoming and outgoing breaths increases. The breathing will become more and more subtle, light and long and one will start feeling more relaxed and peaceful within. Finally, one attains the Supreme State of the all-powerful God-the Universal Consciousness. It is also understood that deep, relaxed and long breathing is an indication of a long span of life.

5. Fix attention on that Pranic, that is, the vital energy that arises from the base of the body, (Mooladhara Chakra is also called the root Chakra or the wheel of energy that is spinning or rotating very fast and intensively like a wheel), like that of the rays of the sun, that gradually becoming subtler and subtler until at last, the energy dissolves in the Dwadashantha Chakra. When the vital energy pierces through each of the Chakras, it will become subtler and subtler and also fainter and fainter. Then finally, it will dissolve in the Dwadashantha Chakra and at that point,

God, the Supreme Consciousness will reveal itself.

The vital energy is supposed to move very fast from the Mooladhara Chakra up to the Dwadashantha Chakra after passing through all the subtle chakras in ascending order.

The Dwadashantha Chakra is supposed to be the subtle Chakra or the subtle wheel of energy that is outside the body and above the Sahasrara Chakra, or the Crown wheel of energy which is the topmost Chakra that is located at the top of the head. The Dwadashantha Chakra is supposed to be 12 inches above our body. The innermost Nadi, that is, the subtle Channel of Energy, namely, the Sushumna Nadi, that passes through the centre of the two central Nadis namely, Ida and Pingala, is supposed to end here. This is also supposed to be the place or point where the breath rests. It is said that the one who fixes his attention at this point will attain the state of Bhairava, the state of Lord Shiva, that is, the state of God or the Almighty. This is because the Pranic, that is, the vital energy that arises from the Mooladhara Chakra (refer to Chakra Meditation in the previous section) gets subtler and subtler and gets dissolved in Dwadashantha, to manifest Lord Shiva, that is, Bhairava, the Supreme, vast, expansive, all-pervading energy or The Almighty. Dwashantha, therefore, represents the highest place of God in the physical body, the vibrating Self.

6. When one meditates upon, that Energy that is moving upwards very fast like a flash of lightning through each of the seven Chakras that are the wheels of one's vital energy, one after the other, up to the Dwadashantha Chakra, then

finally, one will realise the glory of Shiva and will become one with that Supreme Universal Energy and will experience immense Bliss that is the very nature of God.

7. The 12 centres of the 12 Chakras (This technique takes into account 12 Chakras in the body) should be pierced through in a very subtle manner, one after the other, through a clear understanding of the vowels associated with the12 letters of these Chakras (the Sanskrit letters. It is also understood that one can make use of the letters of any other language also, about the 12 Chakras) first in their gross form and later as the subtle sound and still later as mere vibrations using imagination and finally on the silence that is the final stage. With that understanding, one will get liberated from the gross and later all that is subtle and at the end of such an

understanding, the Kundalini energy that reaches the Sahasrara Chakra will enable one to become Lord Shiva Himself or himself.

8. After one's energy is roused and pierces through the various Chakras in the body, one after the other, the energy reaches the Ajna Chakra, which is known as the third eye, the eye of great spiritual Wisdom, and then, beyond that when the energy crosses the bridge between the eyebrows, that is, the Ajna Chakra, and reaches the Sahasrara Chakra that is located (the top most Chakra in the physical body) subtly at the tip of the head, then the mind will lose all perception of dichotomy, that is, all duality of perception, and at that stage, the vast expansive Consciousness-God will reveal itself or Himself.

The Third eye centre where the Ajna Chakra is located is supposed to be a great energy centre. It is said that when the third eye opens up one becomes aware of Himself, that is, the true Self that is nothing but the Soul in him, that is a part of the vast Universal Soul or Consciousness.

The meditation techniques from 5th to 8th are related to Chakra meditation.

9. One has to meditate continuously, for a long period, on the space or void, that is perceived like a peacock's feather that has different colours in it, then, at the end of such prolonged meditation, he will see only that single vast space that is without any dichotomy or colours, and this is the stage when the reality enters into his heart- that void-the Supreme Universal Consciousness or that which we call as God, that is only

one- the Supreme, that is without any other.

The five voids, mentioned here refer to the five senses, namely, the sense of sight, taste, smell, touch and hearing. One is supposed to meditate upon the five coloured circles in the peacock tail or feather by assuming them to be the five senses that are always outward bound. When one starts observing such a feather of the peacock with open eyes continuously, assuming them to be the five senses, then, after some time the circles will start disappearing gradually because the mind will stop thinking about them as they will start disappearing without any thought. That means, the mind will become blank and he will become aware of the Space or Void-The Universal Consciousness and becomes Supreme ultimately.

In the above meditation technique, Lord Shiva wants every being to understand the truth that even though we perceive duality in everything, like heat and cold, sorrow and happiness, darkness and light and so on, in our daily worldly life, still the truth is, actually there is no duality because, in reality, there is only the vast expansive Consciousness, that we, for our understanding call it as God or the Almighty or even as Lord Shiva or by any other name because all mean the same-that is, the vast Universal Spirit or Soul, or Consciousness that is the ultimate Reality that can be only one but not more than one. The duality that we see is not permanent but is ever-changing and therefore is not Real. But the ultimate Superior energy is permanent without any change, is everlasting and imperishable and therefore is the only Reality. This is the ultimate Reality because only that which is permanent can be the truth and the Reality, but not that which is changing and are subject to several modifications. The ultimate Reality can also be only one but not many.

10. Similarly, even if one fixes his total attention not only on the void but even on any other object, for example, a wall, or a person of excellence of his choice, then gradually, his mind will get centred on that particular single object only and he will automatically be able to get absorbed in his Real Self or Soul that is the true reflection of the Universal Self or Soul and he realises and becomes total Bliss- the Supreme Self itself.

The individual Self or Spirit or Soul is the Universal Spirit or God, which is within the physical body of any creation. The Real Self of a being is this individual Soul but not his physical body or mind is only his instruments or tools or the means that enable one to live in this world and more importantly, that help him to reach the ultimate state of attaining godhood.

11 When one closes his eyes and fixes his attention on the inside of the skull, behind the forehead, imagining only darkness there, then gradually, he will be able to stabilize his wandering mind, because then his thought process will start slowing down and there by the numerous thoughts will also start decreasing and a stage will come when he will have no more thoughts except the one on which he is meditating upon, and finally, even that single thought also will gradually disappear and this is the state where the mind merges with the Supreme power -God the Almighty and with such identification, one will

become that-the Supreme Realty or God itself.

12. One may also meditate upon the inner space of the central most Nadi, that is, the vital energy channel, that is named the Sushumna Nadi, which is as delicate as a fibre of a Lotus stem, situated in the central axis,-the Spinal Column and then, finally, by the grace of the Goddess, the Supreme, the Divine will reveal itself.

The ancient Hindu Scriptures state that there are innumerable subtle Nadis or subtle Energy channels in our body even up to several million. In the Scripture namely, Shiva Samhitha, which is an ancient treatise on Yoga, it is said, that there are innumerable Nadis in our body out of which 14 are important and among them, three Nadis are very important. These are, the Ida, Pingala and Sushumna Nadis. The Ida and Pingala run through the centre of our body and the Sushumna Nadi runs through the middle of these two Nadis. The Sushumna Nadi is visualized as a white transparent tube. The Ida runs through the left side of the body and the Pingala runs through the right side of our body. They represent the masculine and feminine energies in the body.

13. When one uses all ten fingers to shut or close or block the seven entrances to one's sense organs in all directions then he will feel that his eyebrow centre is being pierced and light becomes visible there, where the Third Eye is located. By getting absorbed at that point between the eyebrows, the light dissolves by itself, and one realises the Supreme state of Godhood.

The seven openings or entrances mentioned here are the two eyes, two ears, two nostrils, and one mouth. The forefinger is to be used for closing the eyes, the thumb to close the ears, the middle finger to close the nostrils and the ring winger and little finger to close the lips. It is understood that as soon as the light appears, the breath will pause or will get suspended and hence there won't be any difficulty in closing the nostrils.

14. When one presses the eyes very gently, then a subtle light will appear at the top of the head or in the heart region, that is in the form of a dot or Tilak. When one gets absorbed in this, then, that one will experience a condition of agitation and shaking. This will be followed by total absorption of the mind and one will get dissolved (get merged

with) in the Supreme Universal Spirit or Consciousness.

Dissolution of mind is when one's mind disappears because there are no more thoughts left in the mind. At this stage, one merges or gets dissolved in the infinite Universal Spirit or Consciousness.

15. One who is capable of listening intently to the subtle sound (the vibration of sound) that is not openly audible, and which is continuous and uninterrupted in the rushing river or hearing the unstruck sound of the Universal Consciousness-God, the Almighty, by closing his ears, will attain the Supreme State of the Universal Soul as a result of his mastery over Shabda (sound) Brahman, that is, Brahman-the Supreme Consciousness that is in the form of Sound.

In this meditation, one is required to sit with closed eyes near a flowing river, totally engrossed and absorbed in the continuous, soothing sound of the river that is flowing continuously. This absorption will bring peace within himself and gradually all thoughts will start vanishing and one gets united with the Almighty God. He may also focus intently on the unstruck sound of the Universe as a whole, by closing his ears. The great sages or Rishis of ancient India heard many such vibrations of the cosmic sound from Space or void during their prolonged and intense meditation and it is understood that the vibrations from the cosmic Space enabled them to grasp all Knowledge and the oldest scriptures of mankind namely, the Vedas and later the Upanishads and the other ancient prehistoric Indian Scriptures were born.

The ten Cosmic sounds are supposed to be;

1. Bee humming
2. Sound of the word ‘Chini’
3. Bell ringing
4. Sound of conch Shell
5. Sound of stringed instrument
6. Sound of cymbals
7. Sound of Flute
8. Echo of the sound of Drum
9. Sound of two drums and
10. Sound of Thunder,

16. When one is capable of repeating the Pranava Mantra (the sound of ‘AUM’, which is supposed to be the Primordial Sound of the entire Universe) slowly, in a perfect manner, while fixing his total attention on the endpoint of that sound,

its vibration, and the ending silence, for a long time, then, one will be able to get absorbed totally in the silence and thereby will be able to enter into and experience the void- the ultimate Transcendental State of the Supreme, Universal Energy and become spiritually enlightened.

17. The one who can get absorbed totally in the silence, the Void at the beginning or end of the sound vibrations of 'Aum', the Pranava Mantra, or of any letter, gets dissolved in the silence and, as a result of intense and prolonged meditation, he will ultimately become the Void, the Supreme Universal Consciousness.

The void or Space in the entire Universe is filled with Universal Energy or Consciousness. In other words, it is the same as Universal Consciousness. So, the one who gets absorbed and dissolved in the void becomes that void (The Universal Energy), that is God Himself or itself.

18. When one is absorbed in the continuous, prolonged and subtle, vibration of sounds of different types of musical instruments which are strung, or that make use of air or wind and so on, then one will be able to become one with such subtle sound that fills the entire Space that is not audible clearly, then after sometime is not at all audible, and there will be only silence then, finally, that one who remains in such silence will become the Supreme Void or the empty Space-that is, the Universal Energy.

First of all, there will be the sound of the instrument. Then the sound becomes feeble and feeble and the vibrations gradually end and only silence or void remains in the end. At this point, the awareness of the meditator reaches its climax by revealing the Supreme and one gets identified or gets unified with that Supreme, that is, the Universal Spirit.

19. When one meditates upon the void within each of the letters of the Pranava Mantra, by uttering openly or silently, the Bheeja Mantra, -the Seed of all the Sounds, that is, the Pranava Mantra 'AUM', which is the basic or fundamental sound of the Universe as a whole, in a repeated manner for a long period, will finally, in course of time, become the void and attain Lord Shiva by uniting himself with Him, and he will become the very Universal Energy-the Universal Soul by getting dissolved in the Void.

20. If one can contemplate on his body, simultaneously imagining that space or Void is pervading in all directions, within his own body, then in course of time his mind will be freed from all thoughts and finally he will get dissolved in the Space or void that is all-pervading, and that is nothing but the Universal Spirit or God.

21. The one who can meditate continuously and simultaneously on the void above, and the void below his body, will, in course of time be able to go beyond the body consciousness that erroneously makes him think that he is only the body and mind and takes him to the level of becoming Spirit Conscious and thereby attain the Supreme State of the all-pervading Universal Energy, that is, God by becoming the vast all-pervading Space itself that is nothing but the Supreme Soul or Spirit.

22. If one can become watchful continuously for a long period, and simultaneously on the void of his central most Nadi, (the channel of vital energy in the body) that is, the Sushumna Nadi, the void of his base, and also the void of his heart, (the upper part of his body, the lower part of his body and the middle portion of his body) is sure to attain the state of the Supreme Universal Energy, that is, God.

23. If one can contemplate, even for a single moment, any part of his own body as Void or emptiness only, then his mind will be freed from all other thoughts and he will become the very void that is known as Bhairava or Shiva- That is, God with form.

24. One's thoughts will become steady if one contemplates all the constituents of his own body as pervaded by Space

only. Finally, with the disappearance of even that single thought the mind will disappear because that one's mind will get dissolved in the Supreme Consciousness without any trace and at this point, he attains the Supreme State of God.

25. when one meditates upon the skin of his own body as a mere wall or partition, that has nothing within it except space, then, in course of time that one will become like void or space, by dissolving or merging with the very Space-that is nothing but God, the Universal Reality.

26. The one who meditates intensely, with undivided attention and with closed eyes on the Lotus of his heart, (in the heart region) that is, the innermost space of his heart (Which is usually believed by beings to be the location of the

individual Soul or Spirit) will soon become a Spiritually realised Soul.

27. With continuous and prolonged meditation, the mind dissolves in the Dwadashantha Chakra, that is, the subtle wheel of our vital energy that is 12 inches above the head. (The breath is supposed to end here). When the mind dissolves, that is, when the mind collapses without any single thought, then, the true nature, or, the essence of the ultimate human goal or objective will be manifested or revealed in every cell of the body. That means one becomes spiritually enlightened.

When one focuses his attention on the end point of breath, that is, at the Dwadashantha Chakra, then, one's true nature, that is, he, as the Soul is not different from God gets revealed and this Wisdom is the Realisation of the Supreme or God.

28. One may also bring the wandering mind that has innumerable wandering thoughts, again and again, upon the Dwadashantha, as far as possible, so that the number of thoughts starts decreasing day by day. Then after some time, the mind will remain in an extraordinary state always, when it becomes one with the Supreme Universal Realty that is, the source of each and everything in this Universe, that is God or the Universal Energy.

29. One should meditate upon the thought that his body has already been burnt from the foot up to the top of the head, as a result of the movement of Kala, that is Time, and his body is no more. When one contemplates in this manner, then he will be no more body

conscious, but, on the other hand, he will become Soul conscious. He becomes aware of the reality that he is not the body and mind that are perishable in the fire that burns his body after death, and therefore temporary, but the immortal Soul that is imperishable and is therefore eternal. This awareness will make him realise God-the Ultimate Reality.

Kalagni Rudra is another name for Lord Shiva. Kala means ‘Time’ and ‘Agni’ means fire. In this sense, He, Lord Shiva is considered the creator as well as the destroyer of ‘Time’. He is supposed to create and destroy and burn the entire Universe and all the creations in the fire.

30. In the same manner one may also intensely and continuously meditate by imagining and visualising the entire Universe as being burnt by the

movement of time. Then, one becomes a God realised Soul-a Godman, by attaining the supreme state -the state of God that is nothing but the Universal Consciousness.

31. When one fixes his mind steadily and continuously, on the components of his body that are the same as the components of the Universe, (In ancient Indian Spirituality it is said, just as the individual physical body is made up of the five elements of Nature, namely, the Earth, water, fire, air and space, in the same way, in the same proportion, the Universe is also made up of these five elements. This is because according to ancient Indian spirituality, what is true of the microcosm is also true of the Macrocosm. With the death of the person all the five elements in the body merge with the elements that are outside in the atmosphere.) then after a

prolonged and deep meditation on the gross to the subtle and then to the subtlest cause behind the very origin and existence of all creation, including the beings and also the Universe itself, and finally everything disappearing into nothingness, one will be able to realise the Goddess who created the beings (Shakthi or Parvathi that is Energy) along with Her Lord,-Lord Shiva (who is the possessor of Her Energy) and through Her one realises God that is the Universal Soul.

32. After continuously meditating on the energy of all the organs of senses and organs of actions, the mind and so on, one has to fix his mind on the inner space or void in the heart and meditate upon that intently. Such a one becomes a liberated being.

33. Meditate upon the entire form of the Universe and also the course of its development and dissolution, through time and space, and then gradually merge or dissolve until the mind is no more as it merges or dissolves in the infinite, immortal, Universal Consciousness.

In this meditation, one is asked to imagine that the entire Universe is being dissolved from the gross state to the subtle state and from the subtle state to the nothingness that is from the solid, state to the liquid state, then from the liquid state as vapour, and then finally, as Space only, then, at that point the mind gets dissolved by getting free from all thoughts and dissolves itself into the Supreme Power.

34. One may meditate upon the various aspects of the entire Universe and later

as part of Lord Shiva- the essence or the God Principle. Then finally he will realise that he as the Soul is also only a part of God but not different in any way. At that moment one will experience God, - the Supreme Reality.

35. By meditating upon the entire Universe only as Void but nothing else, one will be able to get dissolved in the void- in the Supreme Consciousness by realising the fact that he is neither his body nor his mind but the Universal Consciousness enclosed in his body as the individual Soul or Spirit or Consciousness and he becomes a spiritually realised Soul and becomes the same as the very Universal Spirit or Consciousness.

36. In a similar manner one may contemplate upon the void inside the pot ignoring and leaving aside the structure

that encloses the space inside the pot. After some time, the mind will get dissolved into space, without any single thought, and one attains the Supreme state of all-pervading Consciousness.

The space inside the pot is not in any way different from the space outside the pot because once the pot breaks the space inside the pot becomes the all-pervading Space or void that is the all-pervading Universal Consciousness or God. The pot seems to be different because of its structure and the boundary, just as beings seem to be different from God because of their physical boundaries, particularly, their body and mind. The illusion of difference arises only because of these boundaries. Waves also look different from the ocean because of their physical boundary. once the waves burst then the physical boundary also disappears and what was till then considered a wave becomes the ocean itself. Once the boundaries are ignored, then, there is no difference between the creation and the creator.

37. One may fix his mind on an empty place that has no trees, or, on a bare mountain or any boundaries so that the mind cannot go to any other thought near and around that place. When the mind has no support for any other thoughts, then, in course of time it will get dissolved in that single thought and finally, even that single thought will vanish and that one will experience the Supreme Bliss, -the Universal Truth.

The mind can survive only when there are objects that give rise to thoughts. The vast, clear sky has nothing as there are no objects found there. When there are no objects that can create thoughts, the mind cannot survive because, for its very existence and survival, the mind needs thoughts as the basis. So, without objects, the mind is bound to disappear and get dissolved and one attains the Supreme State by merging with that by realising his true nature as the vast Space -The Universal Soul.

38. Meditate upon two objects at the same time. After some time leave aside the thought of both objects and observe and fix attention only on the gap that is, the space in the centre of the two objects. Then we realise that we are nothing but Consciousness or Soul but not our body or mind because this space or the centre is Awareness or Consciousness. When one meditates in this way, he will come to know his true Nature and is bound to experience the essence, that is, the ultimate supreme Reality.

39. When one can put his total attention on a single object, without having any other thought about anything else, by not allowing the mind to move to any other thought or thoughts, then Awareness of the Supreme Reality will dawn on him automatically.

In the above-mentioned method when one moves away from or leaves one thought, then, he should restrain his mind from moving to another thought. That means he lives in the present moment only but not in the past or future. At that moment, the mind will stop on its own without thoughts by resting at the centre, and in that state, one realises his true nature - the Truth, that he is the same as the vast, expansive Universal Energy that is, the Soul or Spirit or God.

40. If one can fix his attention continuously, with a steady mind, on the entire existence, that is, the entire creation that includes all animate and inanimate creation and also the Universe itself, simultaneously, as nothing but Consciousness or Awareness only, then He will attain the Supreme Wisdom or Awareness that is nothing but the Universal Consciousness.

41. The Yogi who is in the advanced stage of spirituality, that is, the one, who can fuse both Prana, the incoming vital breath with Apana, the outgoing breath either inside the body or outside the body, gets the necessary equanimity of vision, that is, the necessary equilibrium and therefore becomes eligible for realising the Ultimate Supreme Universal Consciousness.

The above method is fully understandable only to Yogis who are in the advanced stage of spiritual practice as it is very difficult to explain but can only be experienced.

42. One may contemplate on the whole Universe or on one's own body that is filled with Bliss of the Self, that is, the Soul or Spirit inside one. Then, by that blissful nature, one becomes the Supreme Bliss itself which is the nature of the Universal Soul.

This is possible only for spiritually advanced beings because only they can be Blissful always with the understanding that one is only the Consciousness but not his body or mind. By that Blissful nature, they become Supreme Bliss itself.

43. One may be able to realise and experience the Supreme Bliss, which is

the very nature of the Universal Soul, by performing religious austerities as well, because religious practises result in great Bliss for the Devotee immediately and this will pave the way for the realisation of the ultimate and permanent joy for the devotee by becoming one with the Almighty God- The Universal Consciousness. (This applies to real devotees who are on the path of Devotion- who surrender themselves to the will of God in an unconditional manner).

44. When all the channels of perception are blocked, particularly, the sense organs, then, the vital Energy in the body will move very slowly upwards, along the Spinal column. At that time, one starts feeling the tingling sensation like that of an ant crawling in the body, and then, one experiences the Supreme

Bliss, which is the very nature or the essence of Universal Consciousness.

When all the windows or doors of the outward-bound sense organs are closed the mind that usually goes outward, through the senses, cannot but turn inward and one will start experiencing the upward movement of the vital Energy in one and this finally results in spiritual awareness or Enlightenment.

45. When one throws away the blissful mind into the fire (the fire here refers to the subtle fire in the subtle Manipoora Chakra, that is, the navel Chakra or the subtle wheel of energy in our body and that has the nature of fire. The inner fire in that Chakra is supposed to facilitate digestion), precisely, into the middle of that fibre-like Lotus stalk (referring to the Sushumna Nadi which is the central most subtle channel of our Vital Energy

that passes through all the seven Chakras) or into that (Chakra, the subtle wheel of Energy in our body) that is full of air (that is, the Anahata Chakra or the throat Chakra), then one gets merged with Bliss- the Universal Spirit.

46. When one gets absorbed in meditation on Shakthi, the energy, then, one experiences union with Shakthi the Goddess, and, in the end, one gets dissolved into the Shakthi-the Energy. The Bliss that results from such a Union, which is supposed to be the very nature of the vast, all-pervading Universal Consciousness, in reality, is nothing but one's Self or Soul or Spirit.

47. One can also experience the bliss of Shakthi, the woman, even in her absence and attain such a Bliss through imagination, and when he gets absorbed in the imaginary union, then the

awareness will dawn on him, that is, the Supreme Universal Consciousness will reveal itself to him.

Tantra is a yogic spiritual practice that is not against worldly life and sex that is the natural fundamental urge along with hunger and thirst for any creation. The desire to appease hunger and thirst and also the desire for procreation we see even in the lowest species of creation up to the highest level. However, one is not supposed to indulge in such worldly pleasures all the time by knowing the limitations and the temporary nature of such pleasures of life. Such knowledge will make one go beyond worldly pleasures and seek permanent Bliss by turning his mind inward and thereby knowing his original nature-that he in reality is the Soul or Spirit but not his body and mind that crave worldly pleasures including sex. This knowledge will pave the way for Spiritual Wisdom, that is, Spiritual enlightenment in which one becomes God itself-The Universal Soul itself.

48. Even if one can contemplate, that is meditate upon the joy that one experienced in any activity, for example, while meeting with close relatives or friends, even then, one through intense absorption of that thought, can experience the great joy that will lead to God Realisation or Bliss.

49. If one fixes his attention on the joy of taste obtained from eating and drinking, then, such a state of contemplation will bring a state of total contentment or fullness and this will culminate in Supreme Bliss, which is the nature of the Supreme Energy.

50. With total attention on the pleasures of the senses like listening to some music, the Yogis also, that is, those who are on the spiritual path, experience pleasures within themselves. When the Yogi gets absorbed in this manner, then he will be able to go beyond his mind and becomes the same as the Supreme Consciousness by merging with that Supreme.

51. Whenever the mind is held back, that is, gets absorbed in complete satisfaction in or from any single thing only, without the slightest deviation, then one will experience the Supreme Bliss, that is the very nature of the Supreme Universal Consciousness.

This meditation technique makes us understand that it is not the object upon which one fixes his attention that is important. The object can be anything, material or abstract, worldly or otherwise. It is the intensity of focusing on a particular aspect, person or object or anything that is most important in meditation.

52. When one enters into that state of sleep that is just preceding deep sleep, that is, at the threshold of sleep when he has neither entered totally into sleep nor is waking, at that junction, juncture, the Supreme Goddess will reveal herself and through Her one attains Lord Shiva, the Universal Consciousness.

In the above-mentioned state one neither is waking nor is in the state of sleep. If one can become aware of this junction point, then Goddess Shakthi will reveal Herself and through Her one attains Spiritual Wisdom, that is, one attains Lord Shiva and becomes Lords Shiva Himself- The Universal Spirit.

53. By fixing one's attention and gazing at Space that appears with different colours due to the rays of the Sun, or even that of an oil lamp, one will be able to realise one's true Self that is only a part or reflection of the Universal Self within one's Self.

In this technique, one is supposed to fix his gaze and attention on the light that seems to appear in different colours from the Sun or from that of an oil lamp. When one observes in such a manner, then, after some time, the colours will disappear for a brief point of time. At that point, when the light disappears the mind will become free of thoughts and it will disappear automatically and the one by transcending the mind becomes the expansive Universal Soul or God.

54. As a consequence of the intuitive perception, of the various Mudras (the

hand gestures relating to the act of worship in Tantra Yoga that brings about a change in the mental makeup of a person. These Mudras are very powerful and as such are to be practised only with expert guidance from an expert master in this field) relating to the Goddesses (The Mudras are, namely, Karankini, Krodhana, Bhairavi, Leilihana, Khekari Mudras) the various forms of the Goddess are revealed and through Her one attain Spiritual Realisation that is Spiritual Wisdom.

In Karankini Mudra one is supposed to imagine and lie down for a long period quietly and without any movement as though he is dead.

Krodhana Mudra is a gesture that shows anger. In this, one is supposed to make his body very tense by keeping his mouth wide open. Then, one is supposed to imagine that he is consuming all worldly objects, notions and also the various ideas about them and then dissolving them totally without any trace.

Bhairavi Mudra is that gesture where one turns his attention inward and fixes his gaze without even blinking his eyes.

Leihana Mudra is a gesture of licking in which one imagines that he is licking away or consuming all dualities of life, that are the opposites of life, like happiness and sorrow, heat and cold and so on, that all worldly beings perceive in the world so that he will never perceive such dualities again in his life.

Khekari Mudra- In this Mudra one is required to roll up his tongue to touch the upper portion of the mouth. It is told that this is the posture of Lord Shiva representing the ultimate Realisation.

That is Spiritual Wisdom or Enlightenment.

55. When one sits on any soft seat steadily for a considerable period, with one buttock and with hands and legs relaxed without any support, as if they are suspended in the space or air, then in that position, the mind is transcended, that is, one goes beyond the mind, and he becomes thoughtless. At that point he attains salvation or liberation that is, he becomes one with the Supreme Energy or Power by realising the Supreme Reality.

The practice of this technique requires the perfect balance of the body. However, one will be able to sit steadily in this posture for a long duration of time, only after a certain level of practice. One will be able to do that, only when his total attention and focus get fixed in the posture, that is, in the present sitting posture.

56. Sit in a comfortable posture and then raise and curve your arms and hands and join them to form a circle over the head, in the form of an arch, and then fix your total attention on the space inside that circle that is, in the space of the armpits. Then gradually the mind becomes peaceful and finally, through that peace one will be able to realise the Supreme by merging with the Supreme.

57. When one fixes his gaze without blinking his eyes and without moving his eyeballs, and also fixes his mind, on the gross or the physical form of any object of his choice, then his mind ultimately will become blank with no thoughts and feelings whatsoever, and at that point of time he will attain the state of Lord Shiva, that means, he will

become the same as Lord Shiva- the Almighty- the vast Universal Consciousness.

If gazing for a long duration of time becomes difficult for the eyes, then, one may close his eyes for a very short while and then open his eyes and continue the practice. However, the mind's attention should be the same as before, that is, without any distractions.

58. When the middle of the tongue is placed in a wide-open mouth by rolling the tongue, where the tongue touches the middle of the palate and if one can fix his attention completely in the mid portion of the tongue, mentally repeating 'HA', then finally, the mind will get dissolved in the Supreme Consciousness-the Universal Energy or Soul.

‘HA’ is the sound of our breath. While practising the above method, it is said, that it becomes possible for one to feel this sound as one inhales and exhales. Gradually, all thoughts will start disappearing and one goes beyond all thoughts, that is, his mind and he will feel immense peace and happiness inside himself. This technique has to be practised by sitting with closed eyes. When the tongue gets tired, then it can be lowered and kept in its usual position for a short while and then after that, this technique can be continued as before.

59. One may imagine and visualise his body, whether he is sitting or lying down, as being suspended in Space without any support. Although the body has weight, one will start feeling that his body is weightless. This will make him go beyond being body, and mind conscious and all his thoughts will start

vanishing and finally, he will attain the Supreme State of Universal Consciousness. Then at that very moment all his inborn tendencies, which are in the form of thoughts, will start reducing. His mind will then longer be the storehouse of his accumulated past tendencies that are in the form of his thoughts first, which lead to his words and actions later. Finally, when the mind loses its support, namely, the thoughts completely, then, there is no mind, and at that moment, one realises the Supreme.

The Yogis who are in the advanced stage of Spirituality and thereby got certain powers, by using this technique were able to levitate their bodies above the ground level, defying the law of gravity that always pulls down anything and everything towards the earth.

60. Even if one gets absorbed in the slow movement of the body while swinging the body, or if one experiences the rhythmic movement of his body in a vehicle that is rhythmically moving, then, one can attain that tranquil state and become Blissful in the revelation of the Supreme Consciousness.

If one can focus on the rhythmic movement and move along with it, then one will be able to remain in the present moment only and will experience calmness and gradually the mind will start disappearing without any thought. Once he can reach this stage then he will experience and become the same as the Supreme Reality itself.

61. One attains the State of Bhairava-the Supreme Lord Shiva-the Universal Consciousness by continuously gazing, even without blinking his eyes, and

fixing his attention on the vast, clear, empty Sky (that has no clouds) and finally, when the Supreme awareness dawns on him, he will merge with the vast empty sky and attains the very nature of Bhairava-The form of Lord Shiva-The Supreme Consciousness.

62. One may also fix his attention on the sky, visualizing and imagining the sky as the form of Shiva, until the form of Shiva gets absorbed in his forehead. Then, finally, one will see only the essence of light entering and filling the entire space, that is, the State of Lord Shiva, the Universal Energy or Spirit and one ultimately becomes that Spirit or Soul.

63. Once a being realises the unreal nature of all dualities in worldly life, like, light and darkness, happiness and sorrow so on and so forth, that he

experiences in his waking state in this world, then, finally, through such knowledge, he will experience the infinite non-dual form of Lord Bhairava -Lord Shiva, the Absolute Universal Consciousness through such knowledge.

The knowledge refers to the understanding that all dualities are temporary and not permanent and therefore, such a perception is not the actual reality, as, what is reality can only be everlasting, non-perishable, permanent but not temporary and only one without a second. Such a being who has this knowledge attains Spiritual illumination- Spiritual wisdom.

64. In the same manner, the one who desires to attain Lord Bhairava, the infinite all-pervading Consciousness, should always contemplate and also

focus upon the terrible darkness experienced during the dark fortnight of the Moon when the Moon is not seen in the sky, and then finally he will attain and will become the same as the infinite Consciousness.

When there is total darkness, one cannot see any object that will distract his attention. He can experience only darkness but nothing else. This will enable him to go beyond any other thought and a time will come when he becomes aware of his Self only that is a part of the Universal Self and becomes that by merging with that expansive Soul or Consciousness.

65. Similarly, one may close his eyes and fix his total attention on the surrounding darkness imagining it to be spreading everywhere in the form of Bhairava. Then, ultimately, he will

attain the state of the Almighty -Lord Shiva and will merge and become that supreme.

When one closes his eyes, he can experience darkness only and gradually gets absorbed in the darkness which ultimately results in his Spiritual Wisdom or enlightenment.

66. The one who can restrain at least the same sense organ continuously, (by not allowing the mind to make the same sense organ function, for example, when the eyes are closed and prevented from seeing anything of the outside world, and revel in the objects that are external or outside of him), will be able to enter the void, the empty vacant space that is beyond all duality and there his Self or the Soul will become illumined and he becomes a realised being- Spiritually enlightened being.

When one shuts all or any one of the sense organs, then, it means, that his mind being unable to see anything external to him, naturally turns inward and then he will understand his true nature, that he, in reality, is the Soul but not his body and mind that are only the accessories or instruments which only help him to reach the final goal of God Realisation. With this Realisation, he attains and merges with the very source of creation- The Almighty God- The Universal Consciousness.

67. By repeatedly uttering the letter Akara, that is, 'A'----- (that is the first letter in uttering the word 'AUM', that can be uttered only when the mouth is wide open) continuously, without any pause or stop, then, at once, there will arise a great flood of knowledge that culminates in the Wisdom of the Supreme God and one gets merged with

the Almighty- The Supreme Reality or the Universal Soul.

The Primordial Sound of the Universe as per the ancient Indian Spirituality is supposed to be ‘AUM’. The very first letter in this is ‘A’. The vibration of the word ‘AUM’ is supposed to be having tremendous power and it is equated with and therefore denotes the vast, expansive Universal Consciousness.

68. When the mind merges with the sound vibration after uttering the last letter ‘M’ while uttering the sacred word ‘AUM’(After the last letter ‘M’, when the sound of the letter ‘M’ is prolonged), without any stop or pause then, the mind will become supportless without thoughts and the mind itself will disappear, that means there are no more thoughts, then, the mind will get absorbed in Brahman, that is the

Universal Spirit or Soul and one becomes the all-pervading, imperishable Universal Consciousness.

One can use the sound of 'M' while he breathes out every time. This can be practised silently and also within oneself or can be uttered openly. The one who intently and continuously focuses on this sound will go beyond the mind, that is beyond all thoughts and will realise the Supreme finally.

69. If one can meditate upon oneself, as the vast, unlimited Space, in all directions, then, after continuous meditation, the mind becomes supportless without the basis or support of thoughts and the mind no longer can survive. At that point the Goddess-Shakthi, that is, the all-powerful feminine Energy will reveal Herself as one's inner Self or the Soul that is the

reflection of the Almighty God or the Vast Universal Consciousness enclosed or present within one's own body as the Individual Soul or the Spirit.

This technique enables one to know his real Self as the all-pervading Consciousness, as the vast, limitless Space or Sky. This realisation makes one go beyond his limited body and mind. At this point, one dissolves into the Universal Soul.

70. One may pierce a little bit, any part of his body, hand or leg and so on, with a sharp, pointed needle or any other instrument. (When any part of our body hurts, immediately and naturally our total attention is bound to get fixed there at that point or place) Then, gradually by projecting one's consciousness there, one will move towards the pure Universal Spirit and ultimately will

attain the nature and the state of the Almighty- The Supreme Universal Soul.

When one focuses on a particular point all thoughts vanish and the mind also disappears, then, finally, spiritual enlightenment happens in a split second intuitively.

71. By fixing one's mind without any diversion of thoughts about oneself or anything else, or on any object, the mind, which is the inner instrument in the body, that is within oneself, will become non-existent without thoughts, becomes empty within and in the absence of thoughts, one becomes free and attains the Supreme State of God- the Universal Energy- the Almighty.

The above technique emphasises the fact that in meditation it is not the object upon which that one fixes his attention that matters but it is the intensity with which one focuses one's attention or his mind that is the most important. In this, one is supposed to meditate on one's body or anything else or upon any object without thinking about its name, form, qualities and so on. But this is very difficult, especially for ordinary beings who are all worldly.

72. Ignorance is the delusive principle that exists in the manifold existence (the world as a whole) that gives rise to name, form and various worldly activities. When we consider the nature and functions of the various elements of nature, (like earth, water, fire, air and space that are also present in all physical bodies of the entire creation in the same proportion performing the same functions) one realises that he is not apart or separate from Nature or Prakruthi (Shakthi, that is Goddess Parvathi) that is part and parcel of the

Supreme Reality. This realisation makes one attain the Supreme Universal Spirit or Soul.

Shiva- Shakthi-, the masculine and the feminine principle depicted in the Ardha Nareeshwara form of Lord Shiva in which Lord Shiva is depicted as half male and half female where the left side of Lord Shiva is His Consort Goddess Parvathi or Shakthi and the right half is Lord Shiva, that shows that the Universe and the entire movable and immovable creations of the Supreme Power, consists of equal parts of feminine and masculine energy.

It is ignorance that makes us perceive and feel that we are all different from each other and also different from God, the Supreme, with different names, forms and also in our mental makeup. All of us and every creation are the same, as we are all a part of the same Almighty. one should be firm in his understanding of this Truth. This understanding will make one Spiritually enlightened with the realisation that one is not actually, his body and mind that are temporary, limited and perishable but the ever-lasting, unlimited, and permanent Soul.

73. One should stop and put an end to all his varied desires whenever they spring up like a flash in the mind (The thoughts of desires that arise in the mind should be destroyed even at that stage when they are like a seed that will sprout and become like a gigantic tree that will be difficult to destroy later) by realising that what all we observe in this world are perishable and therefore are temporary only. When one destroys the thoughts or desires of his mind, then, in course of time the mind will get absorbed in the

very source of creation with the realisation that he essentially is that Supreme power that is only one but not many. With this revelation, one becomes the Supreme Consciousness itself by merging with that source of the entire creation.

74. Having understood the fact through contemplation, one's desires will never give rise to ultimate knowledge that leads to Wisdom, one should start enquiring, "WHO AM I? Am I the body, mind or anything else?" And through such contemplation and enquiry, one will ultimately realise that he is neither the body nor the mind which are only the tools to realise the Supreme, but is essentially the Soul, which is a part of the Universal Soul within his body. This knowledge will enable him to attain the Supreme Power or Energy.

75. When any desire or knowledge arises in the mind then one should imagine himself to be the very Self or the Soul, but not his body and mind, and one should focus intensely on the Self alone but nothing else. Then finally one can realise and become-the Essence, that is, the very God Principle-that is nothing but the Universal Consciousness.

76. The Absolute-the Supreme- the Real Ultimate Knowledge -the Universal Soul or Consciousness has no basis, origin or cause for its very existence and therefore is very difficult to obtain, although everyone knows the relative things of the world, that has a basis or cause behind its origin and therefore are perishable, temporary and so on. Only the Absolute Supreme is the reality, that is the Real and the Ultimate Knowledge, the Universal Soul that has neither any

origin nor destruction, beginning or end. It is imperishable and therefore permanent as nothing whatsoever can destroy it. Therefore, one has to fix his attention on this ultimate truth and contemplate and meditate upon the Real Knowledge- the Absolute Reality only, then, one becomes Shiva Himself- The very Absolute, the Supreme Reality, that is only one.

77. The ultimate Real Nature of Bhairava-Lord Shiva is the all-pervading, undifferentiated Consciousness in all the embodied forms. Hence those who can contemplate upon the entire creation that is enveloped and pervaded by that Supreme Consciousness alone without any difference, will surely be able to transcend the relative existence-the experience of duality and multiplicity that is experienced by the ordinary

worldly beings, and is bound to become all-inclusive and thereby will be able to view all creation the same and as a part of himself and also that of the Universal Consciousness and attain the Supreme by realising the fact that he is the same as the Universal Consciousness as he is made of the same Supreme Energy and with that wisdom, he becomes the Supreme Consciousness itself by attaining that State.

Such a Spiritually enlightened person, will observe all worldly things, dealings and relationships and so on, like a witness, like a mere observer who has no role to play. For such a person everything will look like child's play. However, he will do everything in this world but with no attachment and entanglement. He will be all-inclusive and will see all in himself and himself in all with perfect equanimity of vision.

This is the mark of an enlightened being who has attained God-The Universal Spirit.

78. Whenever negative qualities like lust, anger, greed, delusion, arrogance and jealousy and so on, arise within the mind, then, by using the same mind as a tool one should ponder over such negative feelings and emotions, their origin, their harmful effects and so on. Then, one will realise that only the underlying Universal all-pervading principle, the Essence, - the Universal Soul or Energy is present everywhere, in everything and everyone, and the negative feelings are the result of ignorance or lack of knowledge on the part of one about that Supreme Universal Principle. When one realises this Truth then he will surely attain the Supreme.

79. When one meditates upon the manifest world as a whole as mere imagination, or illusory like that of a magic show or painting, or an illusion and realising the temporary, perishable nature of everything in the worldly existence one is bound to go beyond the world, beyond his mind and body, and attain the Supreme Bliss that is the very nature of the Universal Principle.

When one understands the illusory and temporary nature of the world, then, he is bound to perform all his duties without any entanglement but with total involvement and to the best of his ability. Such a one will also receive everything in life as the same without any preference or prejudice. He will see himself in all and all in himself. He will be quite calm, peaceful, and happy always with detachment and contentment and these are the marks of an enlightened Soul who has become one with the Supreme.

80. The mind should not dwell on the dualities of life like pain and pleasure, happiness and sorrow, and so on. Through intense meditation, one should realise the essence- the underlying principle of all these dualities of life that is in the middle, that is, in between the two opposites of life. Then one will be able to maintain a neutral position in everything without getting affected by anything that goes on around him in the world. Then finally, he will become all-inclusive, by viewing every situation, everything and everyone as the same without any preference or prejudice. Such one becomes a Spiritually enlightened being and attains the Supreme State of the all-pervading Universal Principle and becomes the very Supreme.

81. One should give up one's attachment to his body, which makes him feel that he is the limited body and mind but nothing else. Instead, with intense attention, one should contemplate with a firm mind that he is everywhere and all-inclusive without any limitations and boundaries. Then, one is bound to become all-inclusive, as he sees himself in all and all in himself. This nature makes him experience spiritual Bliss that is everlasting and that is the very nature of the Supreme Universal Soul and he becomes the Supreme itself.

82. One should contemplate upon the analogy of the jar by which one understands that the Soul residing in him is not in any way different from the all-pervading Universal Soul or Spirit, just as the air inside a pot is not different from the all-pervading air outside the pot because when once the pot is broken

the air inside the jar will become one with the air outside. One may also fix his total attention on those qualities that are present within oneself (knowledge, desire and action that are considered the three main energies of the Supreme as well, in Kashmiri Shaivism) but are also found everywhere in the entire creation, in all animate and inanimate creation, then one will become aware of the all-pervasive nature of his Soul, that is, the Soul that is being bound in one's body and mind, and he realises its all-pervasive nature and that it is in no way different from the all-pervading Universal Principle or God. This Wisdom makes him a spiritually enlightened being who has merged his Soul with the Universal Soul- the Almighty.

83. Subject-object Consciousness is common to all, that is, the

Consciousness or the Soul in one and that in another. Usually, the ordinary being considers himself as the subject and another whom they perceive as the object. However, those who are on the Spiritual path meditating continuously are especially alert regarding this relationship. They, the Yogis do not make such distinctions. They see no distinction between themselves and others as they see everyone in themselves and themselves in all. Meditating upon this factor deeply, they can realise that all creation is the same without any difference and they become the Supreme.

84. One has to contemplate upon Consciousness, the Soul residing within one's body, as well as the Soul in another one's body. Then, in course of time, gradually, one will go beyond all sense of limitations or boundaries and

will become all-inclusive and all-pervasive like that of the Universe Soul by realising the fact that it is the same Universal Soul that is present in all creation as the individual Souls and this realisation enables him to see all in himself and himself in all without any difference and this is Spiritual enlightenment that gives rise to Supreme Bliss and one becomes the very Universal Principle or Soul.

85. Through one-pointed attention, one must try to free the mind from all its supports-that means the varied thought processes. When its support, namely, the thoughts get lost, then, the mind, without support or any basis will also collapse on its own and will merge into the individual Consciousness or Soul. At that point, the individual Self or the Soul will become one with the Supreme Self or the Soul and will ever remain in

the state of Bhairava-the Lord- the Supreme Absolute Consciousness.

86. With firm conviction if one contemplates upon the fact that “I am Shiva-The Universal Principle or Consciousness, as I have the same nature as that of Lord Shiva” (because one is the Spirit or Soul but not his body or mind and the Soul itself is a true reflection or part of the Universal Soul or God. So, the individual Soul is the same as the Universal Soul, that is, what we call God) and is bound to get merged with and become Lord Shiva Himself, who is omnipotent, omnipresent and omniscient Universal Principle that is the same as the Universal Consciousness or God.

One, however, is supposed to contemplate upon the fact that in reality, he is not different from God with proper realisation, but not with the sense of ego or the feeling of 'I'.

87. Just as innumerable waves arise from the ocean, and just as innumerable sparks or rays arise from the Sun or the flames of fire or light, similarly, the innumerable sparks of energy of Bhairava- -the Supreme God- Lord Shiva, that emanate from the Lord produce the manifold creation with a part of that energy within every creation as the individual Consciousness or Soul. The one who contemplates this fact becomes the all-pervasive Universal Consciousness by merging his Consciousness with that Universal Consciousness.

88. Whirling the body round and round until it falls on the ground (as in the play of children) making the energy static

one attains the Supreme State of God, the Almighty by becoming motionless.

When one turns his body swiftly, the continuous, fast movement of the body makes him feel dizzy and all of a sudden all thoughts disappear. That means, the mind disappears on its own for a very short moment. When the mind disappears, in that moment of thoughtlessness, the Real, Supreme Truth will be revealed to one.

89. one fails to perceive objects properly due to ignorance which results in a wrong perception of objects that discriminates objects as good and bad. But as a result of intense meditation, if one can dissolve the mind by becoming thoughtless, that is by freeing oneself from all thoughts, then, that one gets absorbed into the Supreme Energy that has no duality and thereby will be able

to see the Supreme God- Bhairava, that represents the Universal Consciousness.

90. Even if one can fix his mind and gaze steadily even without blinking his eyes on any specific thing, then, all other thoughts will vanish and the mind disappears. At such a moment, one will attain the Supreme Bliss that is God by getting united with the all-pervading Supreme Universal Soul.

91. One may close the opening of his ears and also the lower opening, that of the reproductive/excretory organs, in the same manner, and meditate upon the unstruck sound within his body, - the silence, that is without vowel or consonant, and which is the silence within oneself, then one is bound to enter the eternal Universal Consciousness.

When any sound has no vowel or consonant then that means there is no sound but only silence, and in that silence, one merges with God within oneself. In silence, there is no ego either that gives rise to thoughts. Without thoughts, the mind also collapses and one attains the Supreme. However, while practising this technique, one should make sure that no other parts of the body become tense.

92. By standing before a deep pit or well and looking steadily downwards into the deep abyss, without blinking or shutting one's eyes, the mind becomes free of all its modifications, namely, the thought processes, and at once the mind gets dissolved and merges with the Supreme Consciousness.

When one looks into a deep well then, he can see nothing there except darkness and darkness cannot reveal any object and only when objects are there, thoughts will come up in the mind. Without thoughts the mind cannot survive so, it disappears. Then only silence remains and the ego also disappears without the sense of ego that is, the feeling of 'I'. Then, one attains the Supreme Principle-The Universal Soul.

93. Whenever the mind moves outwards or inwards intensely, and deeply, then one attains the all-pervasive state of Lord Shiva because Lord Shiva is the omnipotent, omnipresent and omniscient Energy found everywhere, in everything and every place.

When one sees Lord Shiva as all-pervasive, then he cannot see anything else except the omnipotent Lord Shiva everywhere whether it is outside his body or within himself. He realises the reality that whatever he sees is only a part of that omnipotent God only but nothing else and that there is nothing apart from that Universal, Supreme Power.

94. Wherever the consciousness (here it means knowledge) in one, comes through the organs of senses, for example, through the channel of eyes (When one gains information/knowledge by seeing and observing an object through the eyes), then, by contemplating on that object alone, that is imagined to be having the same nature as that of the Supreme, then, absorption, dissolution and finally, the merger of the mind with the Supreme Consciousness is experienced.

The ornaments that are made by the goldsmith have gold as their basis.

When we trace anything to its origin or base in this Universe, then, we find that each and everything in this creation is obtained from Nature, the Goddess, that is the same as God.

95. The state of the Almighty God, the Universal Soul, one can experience just moments before and immediately after sneezing, or when one experiences terror, intense sorrow, or dissolution due to extreme level of confusion while fleeing from a battlefield, or during intense curiosity, or just after terrible hunger gets appeased. This state is supposed to represent the outward or external state of the all-pervading Universal Soul.

It shows that whenever one gets deeply and intensely absorbed in anything or any situation, then, one attains, by forgetting himself, the state when there are no more thoughts- the mind, and bereft of all the body consciousness he at once becomes Soul Conscious and experiences the Eternal Realty- God-the Supreme Power.

96. One should leave the mind aside and become thoughtless whenever one loses anything that he considers as, near and very dear and extremely valuable to him. In that state of thoughtlessness, the mind collapses as it loses its support or basis (that is in the form of his varied thoughts), for its very existence. This is the juncture when the mind gets dissolved in the Supreme, that is, gets merged with the Supreme Consciousness by losing all its separate individual identity and one attains the Supreme state of Universal Consciousness. This is the state when the individual Consciousness into which one's mind has been already dissolved

losing its separate identity, becomes one with the Universal Consciousness.

97. Whenever one fixes his gaze momentarily upon a particular object, and slowly withdraws his gaze along with the knowledge and impression of that object in his mind, then, gradually, it becomes the resting place of the void that represents the Universal Spirit or Soul. Then only God or void remains and this is the state when one reaches the ultimate state of the Supreme, Absolute Energy-the Universal Consciousness.

98. That intuition that is beyond reasoning, that arises like a flash of lightning, from intense and deep devotion of the devotee who is detached and surrendering to his chosen Deity-the God, is known as the Shakthi or Energy of Lord Shiva. If one focuses his entire attention on such an Energy

continuously, then he is bound to attain the state of Shiva and become the Almighty-the Supreme Universal Soul.

99. When the meditator fixes his attention on a specific object as empty within, for a long period, then, all other objects seem to disappear from his mind and, finally, only the void gets established there. Then, even if that particular object is perceived, he can experience tranquillity and peace within himself, which is the very nature of the Supreme-the Absolute Universal Consciousness.

100. What the ordinary worldly people believe and understand by purity is neither pure nor impure for the one who has experienced Lord Shiva-that is, for a spiritually enlightened being who has experienced the state of the Almighty, that is only one without any duality and

opposites. Freedom from all modifications of mind-that is, the thought process including that of the duality of perception is the real purification through which one can enjoy Bliss -that is, attain the Supreme State of Shiva-the Almighty-the all-pervasive void or Energy.

If anyone sees or considers anything as either pure or impure then that means he has a duality of perception that is not the reality. The duality of perception arises because of ignorance. In reality, there is no duality, as there is only one Supreme that pervades the entire Universe in all objects and beings. The duality of perception will disappear when one starts viewing everything and everyone as the same- as part and parcel of the one Supreme Source.

101. The Lord -Bhairava- Lord Shiva- the Almighty God is present everywhere in every creation as one's Soul or Spirit. By contemplating that, "there is nothing other than Him as He is all-pervasive", one can attain that non-dual State in which one becomes the same as the Supreme without any difference.

When one realises that it is God who is present as one's Soul and that one is essentially the Soul that is the same as God but not his body and mind that are perishable and which are only the instruments to be made use of for his worldly life and more importantly, for attaining the Spiritual Wisdom, which is the ultimate goal of all beings, then one realises that his self is only a tiny part of the very imperishable and ever-lasting Universal Soul, then, he will gain the necessary equanimity of vision in which he will see the entire creation as the same without any difference, even though the creation seems to be varied, and different from each other because of the differences found in their body and mind that are only temporary and perishable. For such a person there is no duality of perception. Such a one is known as a Spiritually enlightened one.

102. The one who does not differentiate between a friend and foe, honour and dishonour by realising and experiencing the all-pervading, Universal Consciousness to be the single all-pervading Supreme Power becomes extremely happy and Blissful that is the very nature of the Supreme State.

This is because he is convinced that the entire creation is only different forms of the same Universal Energy and therefore, he sees all in himself and himself in all, that is nothing but equanimity of vision that is the mark of a Spiritually enlightened person who always enjoys Bliss.

103. The one who treats friendship as well as enmity, (the two extreme opposites that we usually differentiate in worldly life) as the same will always remain in the state of Universal Consciousness by becoming that Supreme Power.

This is because only the one who has realised the Supreme can have such equanimity of vision. For such a person there will be no feeling of attachment or aversion as he always remains neutral without any duality of perception. The one who has such a vision becomes a liberated person even when he is alive.

104. One becomes Spiritually enlightened and wise by contemplating upon Bhairava-Lord Shiva, as totally

void that is beyond the power of grasping or imagined by beings. By fixing his attention in this manner, finally, he realises and attains the state of the Supreme God-the one single Reality-- the Universal Consciousness.

Our limited knowledge is always based on cause and effect. But God, the Supreme is even beyond knowledge, because he has neither cause nor origin, nor the effect that is, the result, like His creation, that has cause or origin and also effect, -the result. That means, God is without beginning and end and is therefore imperishable and everlasting, unlike His creation. He is like a Space that is vast and void.

105. One enters into and becomes the formless, unmanifest dimension-that of the Supreme Consciousness by fixing his mind on the outer space that is

everlasting, - the supportless, the void- the silent, omnipresent and that is beyond all human estimates and calculations.

God the Almighty, the Supreme Universal Soul or Consciousness or Awareness is like Space or Void, that is silent, is all-pervasive and hence infinite, and exists without any support from above or below. With this realisation, if one meditates upon God, as the Void, then he is bound to realise himself- his Self as a part of God that is the true reflection of God- The Supreme Self.

106. Whenever the mind gets immersed in thoughts that bring internal disturbance, then at once one should detect it and set the mind aside. Then, the mind will disappear as it loses its support of thoughts for its very

existence, and gradually one will become peaceful and finally one will enter into the state of Bliss-that is the state of the Almighty God-the Supreme Energy or Power.

Our thoughts are always about the past or future. Once we can arrest our thoughts, then we come to the present where there are no thoughts, thereby there is no mind as well. When the mind disappears Wisdom about the Supreme is obtained by one and he becomes a Blessed and Blissful Soul permanently.

107. The very word Bhairava means, the one who dispels all fear and terror from our minds, who is sound and beyond sound, gives everything to the entire creation, and who protects the entire Universe. So, the constant repetition of the word Bhairava, with this understanding will make one unite with

that Source of creation-the Universal Almighty God- The Universal Consciousness.

A devotee surrenders to God with immense faith and who chants His name always with great humility and with immense trust in God. He is sure that God will take care of one and all, and there is nothing that he needs to do apart from being a good human being. Such a devotee through his unconditional Devotion, faith and surrender to God, is bound to realise and become one with the Supreme State of God, the Almighty.

108. Whenever egoistic thoughts like “I am”, “this is mine” and so on arise in the mind, then at once one should detect and erase such thoughts from the mind by fixing his attention only on the Supreme Power that is the highest Reality. Then

the mind without thoughts will become empty and will merge into the ultimate Reality-the Supreme and one becomes spiritually enlightened.

When one thinks always about the Supreme Universal Consciousness only, without any other egoistic thoughts, then as a result of such continuous meditativeness he becomes Blissful and peaceful, that is the very nature of God-The Supreme.

109. One who becomes meditative always by meditating upon the words (associated with the Supreme Consciousness with their meaning) like 'eternal', 'omnipresent', 'supportless', 'all pervasive', 'Lord of the Universe, and so on, attains fulfilment and contentment by following their meaning. -that is, will realise God-the

ultimate infinite expansive Consciousness.

This is because the meanings associated with these words refer to the Supreme Power and the one who meditates upon these words with their associated meanings as The Supreme, eternal Reality is bound to attain the Supreme- the Almighty God.

110. When one starts viewing the world as illusory like magic that has no essence or reality and becomes convinced of this fact, then, he is bound to go beyond all that is worldly and finally becomes eternally peaceful- Blissful, and attains permanent freedom from all sorrows and sufferings of life - and that is known as Liberation or Freedom, which is the very nature of the Supreme Universal Power.

We, ordinary beings, because of our ignorance feel that the world is a reality. But actually, it is not, because every creation, everything, and every object, including the world and even the very Universe is bound to get perished by the play of ‘Kala’, that is ‘Time’. The only imperishable factor is The Almighty God. When one realises this Truth then he will attain the Supreme that is everlasting and will become that Supreme.

111. There cannot be any activity or gaining of knowledge for the eternally unchanging Self that is within and also all-pervasive. All external objects of the world are bound by worldly knowledge and activity that are temporary and therefore unreal, and therefore the world is also illusory and not real. One should meditate upon this fact and then finally one gets enlightened Spiritually.

Anything perishable can only be temporary. When that is the case, everything in this world, including the entire creation, objects in the world and even the Universe itself are temporary and therefore are not real because what is Real in the Spiritual sense must be everlasting. Only the all-pervading Universal Soul is Real because it has neither origin nor destruction. Everything else goes through the process of birth, growth and decay and as such they are not permanent. Hence one has to fix his attention and attain the Supreme eternal Status of such Supreme Reality only, that is, the very Soul or Consciousness that is eternal and changeless and so on and this is the ultimate goal and objective of human birth, and then, one gets liberated by going beyond birth and death.

112. In reality, there is no bondage or liberation for the Self or the Soul. The permanent Soul is ever free. The bondage and liberation are only for the body and mind which are perishable. If one thinks that he as the soul is becoming free or liberated then it is only wrong knowledge as it is only the projections of the mind like the image of the Sun in the water. One should meditate upon this fact and become spiritually enlightened to attain the state of the all-pervading Soul or Consciousness.

Each being is the soul in him but not his body or mind which are only his accessories and instruments that help him in reaching the goal of Spiritual Realisation. The soul is ever free without any bondage. But due to our ignorance, we do not realise this fact. But when the cloud of ignorance is removed by light, that is, by proper knowledge, then, one attains the necessary Spiritual wisdom and understands this Truth or Reality that the Soul, that is, the Almighty within him is ever free and liberated and there is nothing that we need to do for its Liberation and all our spiritual efforts are only to liberate our attachments to our body and mind.

113. All the windows of perception, namely, the five organs of senses like eyes, ears and so on, through their contact with the objects of the world, bring in only temporary pleasure in the beginning and pain later. Having understood this nature, one should withdraw his senses from the objects of the world by restraining his senses through meditation. Then he will be able to become one with his Soul and attain the state of Universal Consciousness.

When one turns his attention from the outside world and focuses his mind inward, then, in due course he will attain the necessary Spiritual wisdom and attains and becomes the all-pervading Universal Soul.

114. Spiritual knowledge reveals the one single-the ultimate Reality and it is being revealed by one's Self who or which is the knower of everything. One should contemplate upon such knowledge (the Ultimate Reality) and the knower of that (the Self) as the same. (This is because the Ultimate Reality, the Universal Consciousness is also the soul in one) By realising the fact that the knower-the perceiver- the individual Soul which is the subject, and the perceived that is the object of knowing, that is the Universal Consciousness are both the same, one reaches and attains the Supreme state.

After imparting the knowledge of more than 112 techniques of Meditation, Lord Shiva finally tells his Consort- Goddess Parvathi,

"Oh, my dear, when one can dissolve his mind, the intellect, the vital Energy, and the individual limited Self (that does not realise its true identity as a part of the Supreme Consciousness, because of its association with the body and mind)- the set of all these four through meditation, then, the state of Bhairava gets manifested to such a person and he is bound to attain the state of Bhairava- the all-expansive Universal Consciousness".

"The various techniques that I have now revealed to you are meant to help mankind to silence the mind so that they become spiritually wise and enlightened and attain the Ultimate Supreme State even while living. One is sure to get permanently established in the state of Bhairava if he fixes his mind on any one of these techniques and he will attain the power to bless also and whatever he utters will come true. Oh, Goddess, even by any one of these techniques one becomes free from old age, becomes immortal, and also will be endowed with several spiritual powers. He will become the darling of one and all, the most loved and respected, and also the master of all spiritual powers".

In spirituality, it is said that when a yogi reaches a certain level of Spiritual advancement, then he will acquire certain spiritual powers called the Ashta Siddhis (eight types of spiritual powers). Such a being gets liberated even while living.

The Ashta (eight) Siddhis are namely,

1. Anima- the power of making the body as small as an atom;

2. Laghima- the power of making the body light;

3. Mahima- the power to make the body very large;

4. Garima- the power of making the body very heavy;

5. Prapthi- the capacity to reach anywhere that he wants;

6. Prakamya-the power to fulfil any desire;

7. Vashitwa-Control over all objects that are organic or inorganic.

8. Ishitva-the power to create and destroy at will.

The enlightened Yogis will however make use of these powers only for the welfare of the entire creation and the world at large but not to harm any being.

After hearing her Lord, the Goddess remarked,

“Oh, my great Lord, if this is the nature of the Supreme Reality, then one can become liberated even while living and he will not get affected by the worldly activities that he may carry on to fulfil his duties because he will no more be entangled in any of the worldly activities. Tell me, my Lord, in the order of the world in which people worship God, the Supreme with form, name and so on, who should be invoked for, whom one should meditate upon and whom one should gratify through meditation or worship? To whom should one offer oblations, perform Vedic rituals like Yagnas and so on, and how should one perform all these, if we are not different from God?

The Lord replied,

“The various forms of worship are only an outward form of worship meant for the various forms of God. Instead, one may contemplate and meditate upon the all-powerful, all-pervading Supreme Consciousness in a repeated manner, by uttering mentally, the spontaneous Sound of the vital Energy, that is continuously happening within oneself, (while breathing in and breathing out) in a repeated manner, as a Mantra. This is also a form of prayer- This is Japa. Imagining the form of the divine, the Supreme with body, eyes and so on does not constitute meditation. The offering of flowers and various acts of worship is for making one’s mind steady and become focused. Making one’s mind steady in the great Void, without any wandering of thoughts is real worship. From such a worship dissolution of mind will take place. By being established in any one of the above-mentioned practises one attains the Supreme State. When the five elements (that constitute the body of the entire creation as well as that of the entire Universe in the same proportion namely, the Earth, Water, Fire, Air and Space) along with the senses and mind are poured as oblations (this is symbolic) into the fire of the Great Void, (symbolic)- the Supreme Consciousness, using the individual Soul or Consciousness as a ladle, (as in the Vedic Sacrifice) then, such a ritual is characterised by Bliss and then one attains the Supreme. In this system (Kashmiri Shaivism) this is the real meaning of Vedic Sacrifices (Known as

Yagnas). One's Self or Soul, in reality, is the all-pervasive Supreme-the Bliss-The All-pervading Consciousness. Real purification is the absorption of the all-pervading Universal Soul into one's Soul, which is the same as the Universal Soul. Ultimately, the worshipper, the worshipped and the act of worshipping become the same without any difference. This is the Supreme State and destination of one's Spiritual Pilgrimage. The essence of one's Soul is Freedom, Bliss and Consciousness. When one immerses one's limited Self (the lower, emotional mind) into his True Self (the Soul that is also the Supreme all-pervading Soul partaking in all its glory), then that is real bathing-real purification. In such a state who can worship and whom to be worshipped?"

"The breath, the vital Energy, the Goddess Shakthi (energy) goes out and comes in, in a curved manner forming a circle. One has to focus one's attention on Her. She goes far, up, and down. One has to reach Her and that is the real Pilgrimage. The breath is exhaled with the Sound 'HA' and inhaled with the sound 'SA'. In this manner, each repeats the Mantra "HAMSA' even in an unconscious manner".

(The word 'HUM' in Sanskrit means 'I', and the word 'SA' means 'THAT'. Together it means 'I AM THAT' or 'I AM GOD'. 'HAM', that is, 'I' here refers to oneself - one's Soul and 'Sa' refers to the all-pervading Soul of the Universe-God, showing that every creation in essence, as the Soul, is the same as the Supreme Principle-God. One may also hear the sound 'SO' while breathing in and the sound "HUM" while breathing out. Together it is 'SOHAM' that means 'THAT'

(Referring to the Universal Consciousness) and ‘HAM’, that is, ‘MY SELF’ or SOUL’. Together it means ‘THAT’ referring to the Supreme Soul, is ‘MYSELF’. So, whether it is ‘HAMSA’ or ‘SOHAM’ in both these, the meaning is the same. It is understood that each one of us on average, repeats this mantra (breathing), 21,600 times throughout each day and night-throughout 24 hours on all days and nights, from our birth to death without any stop).

“Fire, that is, the Energy that is Goddess Parvathi, is full of great Bliss. By following Her and getting identified with Her one attains Her and then through Her one attains God- Lord Shiva- The Supreme Consciousness. This meditation, however, is not at all difficult for anyone except for the ignorant ones”.

"Oh, Goddess, I have so far explained to you the Supreme Teaching that leads one to the Supreme State of immortality."

(One becomes immortal when one goes beyond birth and death, and attains and becomes the same as the all-pervading Consciousness).

"My teachings should however be disclosed and imparted only to those who are spiritually inclined and who are eager to become spiritually realised and therefore enlightened and wise. It should not be imparted to people who are wicked, cruel, and who are unfaithful to their master who imparted this knowledge, and so on. On the contrary, these teachings are to be imparted without any fear to those whose minds are free from any doubts, who are devoted to their lineage of masters, one's race, family, nation and so on. All worldly belongings are temporary but this supreme wealth is the real wealth that is everlasting and that leads to the Supreme nectar of immortality and it should never be given to people who do not deserve this Supreme Wisdom".

After listening to Lord Shiva intensely, finally, the Goddess said, "Oh, God of Gods, now I have understood the essence of the 'Rudra Mala Tantra' and all my doubts are cleared and I am completely satisfied."

Having stated this, Goddess Shakthi-Parvathi, embraced Her Lord in great happiness.

(Rudra yamala Tantra which contained 64 chapters, is one of the most important ancient Sanskrit Tantric texts on Kashmiri Shaivism. The original text seems to have lost now. They are found only as quotations in later writings. This book is supposed to be the source for later Tantric writings. Vigyan Bhairava Tantra is supposed to be a part of this book).

In this way, Goddess Parvathi- Shakthi, understood the essence of the ultimate Reality from Lord Shiva and later, through Her as the medium, this great Spiritual Wealth was passed on to succeeding generations.

OM

NA MA SHI VA YA

www.ingramcontent.com/pod-product-compliance
Ingram Content Group UK Ltd.
Pitfield, Milton Keynes, MK11 3LW, UK
UKHW041635190726
13854UKWH00006B/2514

9 798890 028402